Did Someone Say Tomorrow?

Mark Howard Bowles

To Susan Yvonne

Who loved me true for a quarter of a century.
May God give you much joy in this life and the next.

Published by Purpose International
Library of Congress Catalog Card Number: 95-92351
ISBN: 0-9647024-0-1

Photographs by Mark H. Bowles

Printed in the United States of America
by Printing, Inc., Wichita, Kansas

June 1995
FIRST EDITION

Cry heart, cry for the adventure that you
have known.

Cry heart, cry for peace you knew once
and the place you knew it.

Cry heart, cry for the intrigue of nature,
the small-the large, the old – the new,
the now – the then –

Cry heart, cry for what you have known
not for what you are.

Cry heart, cry for the experience of the
mountain top and for what you
learned there – a glance from where
you came and to where you go.

Cry heart, cry for all you have seen, the
high – the low, the beautiful – the ugly,
the hurt – the serene and be glad
that all that is, is.

Cry heart, cry for me, for I have know,
I have seen, I have been to the mountain
top but I have not
understood.

Cry heart, cry for yourself, for the
world and her ways pass even
before your eyes in an endless
parade of what is and what will be,
but even you do not perceive.

- Joe Nix
Jan 15, 1970

Contents

Table of Contents

I

Table of Contents *(cont.)*

Table of Contents *(cont.)*

Table of Contents *(cont.)*

Table of Contents *(cont.)*

Table of Contents *(cont.)*

Table of Contents *(cont.)*

Table of Contents *(cont.)*

VIII

Table of Contents *(cont.)*

IX

Table of Contents *(cont.)*

Prologue

Prologue

I guess what I should tell you is that when I was a kid I had my bottom dresser drawer chock full of poems. For better or worse, many of those "bottom drawer" creations are contained in this volume. Consequently, some of this work will seem juvenile, sanctimonious, fatalistic and uninspired. Some of it is. Nevertheless, I'm throwing in a smattering of all. Bringing this volume to fruition has been almost a lifelong ambition. If it is not a literary accomplishment, at least it is one of determination.

Growing up in the isolated, repressed Delta, we sometimes had little more than our imaginations and dreams. This work is somewhat of a chronicle of my own life, of acquaintances, of the generic human dilemma. The emphasis is more on evocation of feeling than on clever heuristic explorations. Sometimes, I'm speaking for others about things I can hardly know. Some things I do know about – medicine – I have largely withheld for a later time, for reasons of sanctity and propriety.

For simplicity, I have chosen to arrange these writings alphabetically and, thus, there is no chronological or intuitive sequence. I am privileged to include some poetry by old friends.

On a personal note, I suffered major losses in the last few years. As a sort of catharsis, I am sharing my thoughts; and going forward with the second half of my life in healthier, more constructive and helpful ways.

I wish to acknowledge friends without whose help and encouragement this book would not have come to fruition. Predominant among them is Donna Hill, who transcribed this work and constantly urged me to follow through.

I thank Dr. Johnny Wink for his editing skills. Special thanks to Dorothy Oyer and Ernie Castro for literally saving my life. Love to the following who gave me unfailing support in dark times: Debbie and Dan Holloway, Delmar Oyer, Tom and Diana Cain; Frankie and Katie Bates; Tommy and Linda South; Rev. George and Arlene O'Neel; Betty and Emerson Paulsen; Steve and Jeanette Grantstein.

Thanks to the following for sharing their experiences with me and helping me to believe that I could go on: Sherlyn Delaney, Kathy Benzing, Debbie McClanahan, Michael Christian and Nancy Stiffler. I thank Chuck Knowles who helped me understand that God is always in control, even when his purpose and plans are unclear.

Thanks to Rev. Roger Roberts for sharing important scriptures; to Dennis Oyer for his exhortation and spiritual wisdom; to Bill Stites for his loving confrontation.

Thanks to Virginia Edwards, J. O. Powell, Virginia Herren and Maude Maddox, my English teachers, for encouragement in the early days. Thank God for enduring friends like Judy Merriman and Margaret Lamar.

Thanks to my sweet mother, Berlin, who always loves and prays for her children, no matter what. Thanks to my sister, Dawn, who has taken many heavy steps with me.

Thanks to my nephew, Clayton, who held me up in prayer and reframed things to give me new perspectives. Thanks to my cousin Linda for listening. Thanks to Justin Autumn and NoraLee, my beautiful daughters, for struggling through all of it. I'm sorry. I love you. God bless you.

Mark Howard Bowles, M.D.
President, Purpose International
1215 N. Emporia
Wichita, KS 67214
May '95

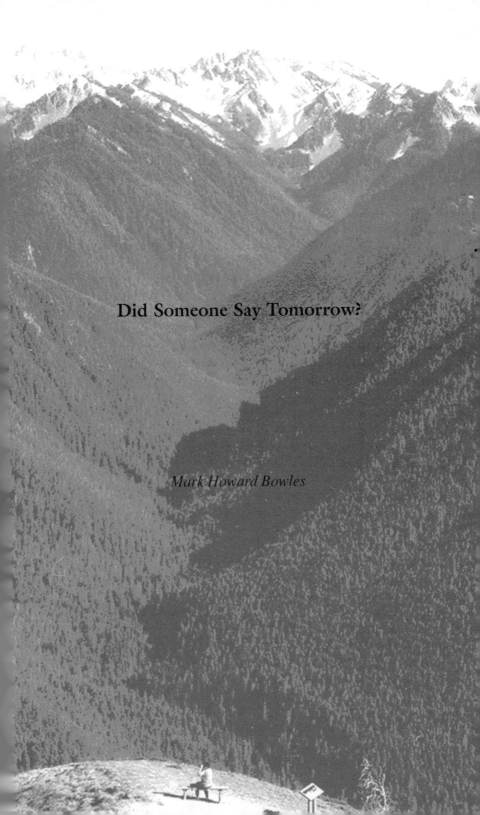

Did Someone Say Tomorrow?

Mark Howard Bowles

1968

I don't condone euthanasia; neither do I condemn it.
It is another of those nebulous issues. Without having
experienced the dilemma of a loved one dying of an
irreversible disease, it is difficult to predict my conviction
or recognize my present feelings.

It would seem that there are two basic issues concerning
the main issue:

(1) Definition of life — Is life the totality of mercy -
Let man mercifully relieve pain or let nature take
its course which could be very painful?

(2) Medical morals versus civil law — what does civil
law rule when a physician preserves life or mercifully kills?

Such questions are not easily answered; much less are the
answers agreed upon.

A Car's a Rollin' Coffin

A car's a rollin' coffin,
    A lookin' for a grave
And those who fill its chamber
    Would have to be most brave.

Some people do their trav'lin'
    In coffins, with white pills;
But I will do mine walkin'
    And take mine without wheels.

A Legacy

When there's no rage
against death
He swiftly comes and
takes our breath
The breath that God
gave man to breathe
to use to laugh and
not to grieve

To compliment not
criticize
To make amends and
sympathize
to praise his name
not curse and swear
to say **I can I will**
I dare!

A New Dawn

Weary legs trudging along,
Heavy hearts without a song,
Swollen eyes, all, full of tears
And worried minds, deluged with fears.
Bleeding feet brown with dust,
Wrinkled hands orange with rust,
Ringing ears all deaf to sound,
bludgeoned heads bent toward the ground.
Shoulders stooped without a load;
Bloody prints along the road.

A blackened night of living dead,
A table full of stale bread,
An inky sky of faded stars,
and... Wait! a faint-gold glow afar!
That must be why they all have gone:
A ray, a hope, a new dawn.

White Mountains, New Hampshire

4

A Prayer of Thanks
1963

We thank thee O Lord
For thy blessings and love,
For the truth of thy word
and nature's glories from above.
We thank thee for
    expansive fields
Of golden grain,
For depthless skies
And infinite plains.
We thank thee for rain,
For storm and snow,
That fall beneath thy feet
Onto this sinful world below.
We thank thee for the blue
    of the sea

Hurricaine Ridge, Washington

That meets the golden sky,
Just between the light and darkness
Of dusking day and dawning night.
We thank thee for stars up in the sky
That twinkle back at our wistful sighs.
And too, the sun at its early rise
That lights the earth and darkened skies.
So is thy love
Which brightens the darkened heart of man
And brings him out of the miry clay
To righteous life again.
O my Savior,
Who could doubt thy creation,
The universe thy hands have sod?
I know for sure it took more than a man.
It took a god, my God!

5

A Single Jonquil

A single jonquil rose
An act of bravery
In beauty bright it smiled
But no one looked to see.

The stately elm rejoiced
His April cloak was new
But none admired
    a single leaf
For they had deeds to do.

But I, I saw the flower
And reveled in its smell
I heard the robin sing
    his song
And saw each leaf as well.

Asheville, North Carolina

The jonquil lay today
All trampled in the grass
One did not see its smile
Now none will as they pass.

Today the robin's breast
Is red with quiet blood
Since one has stilled his throat
He is misunderstood.

Today the tall green elm
Lies still, no arms, no head;
Now there will be no shade
No sigh for those who wed.

And suddenly a silent tear
Crept softly on my cheek
And for a while I sat in quiet
And could not hear or speak.

6

A True Friend vs. Regressive Tradition

A true friend: one who calls you long distance without wanting/needing anything from you.

The ultimate insult: someone invites you home to dinner and then, unexpectedly, orders in pizza.

Poorest manners: a lady lipsticking and brushing her hair at the dinner table after a meal.

Also ran: older gentlemen who smoke up bathroom stalls and then don't flush; who hock and spit incessantly; who let their fingernails grow ungodly long or else clip them during a public meeting.

Unbelievable: loud noseblowing with a careful check of the handkerchief afterwards (for what?). Then with a different part of the hanky, calculated reaming of both nostrils with, of course, a check on the products. And then that all goes into a pocket and the guy extends his hand to greet you.

Why do those little old ladies always carry kleenex rolled up in one fist, stuck inside their waist or down in their bosoms? What do they use it for? Do all little old ladies have allergies or sinus problems? Is this a holdover from the old days when men needed hankies to wipe away tobacco juice from the corners of their mouths and little old ladies needed to wipe the drip of snuff from their chin? Were these people real druggies back then? Men and women addicted to tobacco? How did they ever kiss with all that in their mouths? Why did they have such overwhelming oral needs and needs for pharmacologic stimulation?

A *True Friend vs. Regressive Tradition (cont.)*

Why do older women spend so much time/money on their hair and let their bodies go? Why do they wear so much makeup that their skin can't breathe?

Of course hankies also help to mop the beaded brow, slaving, so to speak, over a hot stove.

And grandma doesn't think twice about spooning out the full-strength mayonnaise, frying with Crisco or toast-sopping up an egg yolk. But, she's had ample opportunity to read the same things I have. God knows that a layperson can't help but be informed today. So why is change so difficult? Why are new actions so revolutionary? How does one factor out things and hold onto the thrice-used kleenex? Why can't progressive change be as secure as regressive tradition?

Pizza-in is a regressive tradition. Thank you very much for the thought.

Aborted
(Summer of Mercy, 1991)

Wriggling,
 withdrawing;
  and screaming inaudibly
   as an unsolicited infusate converts
    the physiologic milieu into a
     hypertonic cistern of
      doom.
Choking,
 sputtering,
  convulsing yields to irreverent silence.
   Though the heart rests, the soul is aware
    of the rupture, dismemberment
     and destruction of its
      physical habitat.

The scream joins a
 tenor din of
  countless voices
   penetrating eternity
    forever.

Markham St., Little Rock, Arkansas

10

All My Life

All my life
People been breakin' my heart,
All my life
I been waitin' a new start.

But it'll probably never come
For as long as I live,
'Cause a man keep the skin
That the good Lord give.

Yeah, I been waitin'
For a long, long time,
And I say
Yeah, I say it's a crime:

When a man hate another
For the color of his skin,
He gonna answer to the Lord
'Cause I tell you it's a sin.

When I cross over that Great Divide
and lookin' back from the other side–
Well, there won't be no sadness,
              no tears on my face,
       just a poor, sad-sick sinner
              saved by God's grace.

Alone

The door closed the laughter inside.

The cold of the night brought loneliness back,

a faint ache in my mind.

I walked a little hunched,

smiled a sadder smile.

Everyone else inside, with the smoke

and the warmth and the long stories;

And I outside with silent stars.

An Expression of Dislike

If I could only thrust all my hate
into your ugly indifferent heart
in one jolting, violent stab,
I would do it with alacrity.
I would cut out your cold eyes and
let my children play marbles with them.
I would mount your nose on my wall
above a cuspidor of rotten garlic and let
your soul seep in that stinking hell for a thousand
years.
I would cut off your ears and throw them
in the subway tunnel
so you might hear the stream of humanity which
you so long and callously ignored.
You are a bastard
Conceived by a shrew in a pit of snakes.
I would pull your tongue out by the roots
and throw it in the deepest ocean
and forbid it to ever rise again above
the pounding surf and roaring waves.
I would take your hand, mount it,
and put it in the garage we abandoned 20 years
ago.
There in the dark places where those hands
were always grasping, groping, gripping
at my eternal being, reaching for my very soul,
clutching my life. But no more...
I shall throw your limbs to the dogs (mongrels)
and watch them puke you up for a week and a half.
I hate your gory guts, I hate your glutton desires,
I hate your greedy mind, you whore,
you devil, you demon, you infidel.
God hates you too!

And As I Bend Down

And as I bend down

    to pick up rotten

      shoelaces

And nursery rhymes

    thrown out the backdoors

      of children's lives

I look up at the colorless

    skyscrapers

      and cry

And I shall pray that
love will be yours as
it has been mine
and that the winter
sun will not set
in the empty fields
until you know
what it
means to
share as well
as to give.

———————

Your words lodged in my right temporal lobe
precipitating an occlusion.
I guess I let you go to my head.

———————

Gracie Grunt dreamed that
Greta Cudie
Saw Damar Varnish
Doing his duty.

15

And Love...

And love comes bounding down
                           the street

And love flies swiftly through
                           the air

And love makes people run
                           and laugh

And sometimes...
                           love whispers.

And the Birds Sang

and the birds sang
and the birds flew
as J.F.K.
came riding through
the sparrow must beware of the lark
the robin hides in the hills after dark
the butcher bird waits with thorns for
                    the king
and the blue bird can tell you
                    everything

And We Run

And we run to be ourselves
somewhere where the flowers grow
never planted by man –
but the sun is going down
and we always have too far to run.

Crescent Lake, Olympia National Forest

And You Will Know The Work
and the Work Will Set You Free

When I was young, and not so old,
When I was dreaming of skies untold
The rings of Saturn, canals on Mars
When I was vaulting among the stars.
In open meadows, in fields of green
kissed wind-swept clouds,
Unheard, unseen;
From tawny sunsets to inky nights
Without a fear; without a light
When I was young.

Then later on, when older still,
I had a thirst I could not fill;
Indomitable passion for toil and power
had brought me to a later hour.
Achievement was an opiate
That only work could satiate.
I sacrificed my family
And made them low priority
When I was older, older still.

Then later on when I was old
No love for silver, no love for gold;
Prestige and Presence well assured
But agonies that can't be cured
When I was old.

Anonymity

Count up the dead and say they died,
Not how they fought and how they tried
To save your life and mine.
Don't give their names, it's useless say,
For time obscures them anyway
And there are more in line.

So say, "Our casualties were light"
Or else forget there was a fight;
Say dead men there were not.
And someday then you'll think what's said
And pity not that they are dead
But, worse still, forgot.

Anonymous Letter

"Hello kid; hope this letter finds you OK., as for me I'm alright . . . Linda wrote and told me that you and her and Johnny and kids and the man with the broken heart, all went up to Eagle Lake . . . Man, I sure do miss y'all, it's something like being dead, being in this place.

. . . I was glad to hear you got off those dolls, maybe now you can write me more. It gets lonely as hell here and the only thing that helps is a letter.

. . . What did you think about Kennedy getting zapped? I thought it was a pretty rotten thing to do. I don't know what this world is coming to. Instead of being America the beautiful, its more like America the sick. They say we have a democratic government, I wish someone could show me where to hell it's at. The President is chosen at a hardware shop. The ability of a candidate to win an office is not by winning the majority of popular vote, but is decided between the crosshairs on a rifle scope. And what is the baloney about freedom of speech? John F. Kennedy, Robert K. and even Martin Luther King just expressed their ideas for a better nation. They didn't appeal to somebody, so someone just got them out of the way, 'The democratic way.' "

April 1, 1967

While crawling through some undergrowth
A Viet Cong I chanced to meet.
A greasy mop grew on his head
And PF sneakers on his feet.

He looked at me with puzzled air
As if to say I'd done him wrong
And in an oriental tongue
He asked "are you a fellow Cong?"

I laughed at him with hearty voice
And said "Be on your way.
I'm neither Viet Cong or foe
For this is Labor Day."

"Ha so!" he said, " let's celebrate"
And took a shot of dope.
He even offered some to me
But I replied just "nope."

So here we were or there he was
And I kept playing cool,
Then raised my gun and shot the guy
And hollered "April Fool!"

April and My Life

April's gone and lost forever
Having offered twenty showers
(One for each year of my life)
Prelude to diminished powers.

Arbitration

The attorneys hammer out proposals, counterproposals
and compromise as I sit in the waiting room.
The Lord is my shepherd...
"They want more money."
I shall not want.
"She is concerned that you will get mad and not pay
the kids' college education."
He maketh me to lie down in green pastures...
"They want you to assign $200,000 of your life insur-
ance to alimony coverage."
He leadeth me beside the still waters
"They want ten years"
He restoreth my soul
"She wants you to continue half the alimony payment
even if she gets married."
*Yea, though I walk through the valley of the
shadow of death...*
"Let's hope she does marry him!"
I will fear no evil.

Ascertainment in Courtroom #4
9-11-93 Birmingham, Alabama

After broiled mackerel, squash croquettes and pecan pie in the courthouse cafeteria I went up to courtroom #4. I sat in the front row with the reporters.

It seems that "Killer Joe" by reputation of Fulton Co., Georgia, was on trial for slipping a quadriplegic, porphyric, intubated Robert a fatal windfall of lidocaine so his heart would conduct nothing through its electrical system.

Seems he liked the thrill of Code Blue, so if patients were doing too well he tended to stir up something, so to speak. I had the blasphemous notion, as I sat behind him, that he was looking at the forensic pathologist on the stand and thinking, "Boy, would I like to resuscitate you!"

See he really didn't mean no harm, honey, just 1,500 mg instead of a hundred and the guy really didn't need *any*!

You see, Joe's modus operandi was well-suspicioned by hospitals in Georgia but better to fire him on some application technicality then to raise a ruckus about him killing patients. Why, wouldn't every family member that ever had someone die at that hospital be gunning for this dude? and the hospital? They might be found negligent in not having checked this guy out enough.

I noticed he (Killer Joe) had a tic (his head bobbed around) and I wondered whether that was new or old and the gal sitting next to me from the Atlanta Constitution didn't know. Unusual in a young (35 yo?) man, but they didn't know of any premorbid psycho history.

Ascertainment in Courtroom #4 *(cont.)*

Judge Pearson was a large black man with an effete demeanor appropriate for his judgeship. I never saw him change position. He dismissed the expert witness and jury no less than 4 times to wrankle with the defense attorney, who was slow and deliberate and sometimes less than inspired.

At one point the judge gave the analogy of the organs all being thrown into one bag for toxicological investigation as mixing "the grits into the gravy." He quelled any stereotypical views by quickly adding that he never ate grits. Boy, was I relieved!

So Robert, the patient, had this seizure, presumably from Lidocaine, and then his heart stopped, was jump-started briefly a few times with adrenalin and then was quiet. Two doctors were there at the time so it doesn't sound like Joe, the nurse, really got much action except vicariously.

Demographic studies at other hospitals had shown the only statistically significant factor associated with cardiac arrests was the presence of Joe, the death angel, on the shifts. It is surprising that the fellow got this far, this long, unscathed. Maybe he saw Kathy Bates in Misery too many times (she was a nurse kid-killer) or followed the lead of a "mercy nurse" in a Minnesota VA hospital from some time ago.

I don't understand why Joe wanted to give such industrial strength doses of Xylocaine if he just wanted to have a little fun. Any nurse should know toxic from lethal. Toxic range is a level of > 6 and this man's level was 99.9!

Ascertainment in Courtroom #4 *(cont.)*

I got to meet the victim's family on the way out. I offered Mrs. Price some servile, inane platitudes such as, "I know this has been hard for you" (since March 91) and "God has a way of working these things out." Sometimes I wish I could just keep my polite southern mouth shut and let people say what they want to say. She was nice as she could be though she seemed embittered by the long struggle– so long to bring the alleged perpetrator to trial, and then, who knows, if to justice.

It let me see again how doubly hard we hold onto the soul and spirit of a loved one when their body is slipping away. And why not "Keep hope alive" as Jesse Jackson says? These decisions of omission of life support are hard enough for families and usually occur long after the attending physicians have concluded there will be no recovery. To move from that timid step to a direct act to shorten life seems not only unthinkable but highly unlikely for the usual loving, agonizing family.

In this way, "Killer Joe", if guilty, is an affront to us all and the sanctity of life. He is like a mother exchanging her nursing breast for a pacifier dipped in strichnyne. It is like sitting on a commode and having something come up out of the water at you. To sign up for compassion and healing and to receive an unconscionable boost into eternity is unthinkable.

As I stepped onto the elevator, I closed my eyes and reached out and touched the braile. For just a moment I thought of Robert and what it would be like to have my fingerpads burned away.

Awaiting the Train
by Wayne Winkle

I stand on the platform waiting for the train,
All around me jostle the life-blood of our nation.
Young men, waiting also for the train.
Young men who are leaving for war
With the spring of youth in their step.

Pity, young men, pity.
That is what I have for you.

I once stood on this platform,
Waiting for the train to take me to war
I once had the spring of youth in my step;
Then the train came
And took me to war.

Now I am here again,
Waiting for the train that will take me home.
I lie here peacefully,
Awaiting the train.

Awake! My Son

Awake! My son, the sun is up
And fields are fit for plowing.
Awake! your coffee's in your cup
And all the horses bowing.

Awake! My son, it is the noon;
The land is set for planting.
Awake! the lunch is ready soon
And all the mules are panting.

Awake! My son, the night is near;
The crop is ripe for reaping.
Awake! for suppertime is here —
But no, my son, keep sleeping.

Carpathian Mountains, Romania

AWOL

She said she knew Kenny
    and once dated Paul
She said she had friends in Big D
She said she had children that
    stayed with their father
Whenever she came to Tennessee.

She said she lived down in South Arkansas
And sometimes she had to get away
As she kicked off her shoes
    and lay on the couch
With tears well I heard her say...

Oh what a beautiful night
Oh what a beautiful night
Oh what a beautiful night
Oh what a beautiful night.

Bane and Respect

There was a man
Named Mr. Bane
Who constantly
Was raising cane
About the drought
Or else the rain.

He scorned the rich
For having wealth,
The poor for not
Helping themselves,
Well everything
Just right and left.

Another man,
He named Respect,
Found good in all
Of all effect
And on the right
Did he reflect.

He praised each thing
That met his sight
And said the wrong
Might too be right.
Respect, he held
A blinded light.

Bane and Respect *(cont.)*

Now each of these
Goes to extremes,
From stretched reality to dreams
And each is bad
To me it seems.

To criticize
Makes no one great,
The one whose baned
Or he who say't,
And furthermore
It stirs up hate.

Now flattery
Not from the heart
Doth breed misgivings
From the start
Until it tears
The two apart.

The level-head,
Now look at him:
His world is neither
light or dim
And he can pity
Both of them.

Be Mine Sweet Words Today

O divinest, noblest form of man,
To thee and thine be mortal praise;
But now exalted, you lay deaf,
and blind to marble shrines we raise.

O forbid it God that I be famed in death
When music is a distant din.
Ay, let those flowers bloom while I do live
And let me hear sweet words of men.

O may I have eyes to see and ears to hear
While blooms the blossom of my days;
So I will not regret that coming hour
When Death will take my life away.

O then I shall be content to die
And laugh at Death all clothed in gloom.
Yea welcome him with dancing eye
And enter willingly my tomb.

Beginning Again

You are still the major measure
of my happiness. The very heart of God
knows I love you most
      and only.
The soft lapping of
the waves at the pier
reassert this one fact:
      I love you, I love you, I love you....

The chimney swift circles
an invisible net around an
inescapable realization:
      I am yours forever.

Therefore let us begin the
mutual eternity that God has
ordained. We should not look back.

Tuscan, Arizona

34

Beauty Unseen
1959

This morning I awoke before the dawning
As every morning
I listened to the blue jays scorning
in the tall trees.
The squirrel rustling in the red oak leaves
The rooster and his morning call
as he perched on the old horse stall.
— Then the sun rose over
The distant hills
casting its rays across the fields
of golden grain,
shining its beams of silver
made the darkened stream a jeweled river.
And again
a new day was born
a wonderful sunny morn!
I got out of bed.
No longer would I rest my head
for why let a beautiful sunrise dawn
And me be with closed eyes.

I found my trusty cane
And set out on a walk
down the old path again
to hear bright beauty talk.
The wind blew about me
as I walked along
And as it whistled I thought
it sounded like a song.
It was good to feel the wind;

It's touch is like a silent friend.
The dirt beneath my heavy feet
like drums beat to my every step
a silent tune.
I marched on
along the winding path, a song
in my heart.
The music was majestic trees
swaying in the morning breeze.
Atop them were the little birds
chirping, chirping unknown words
to each other.
A pattering of tiny feet
as a rabbit goes bounding off
into the field of golden wheat.
And now I come to the river
its waters as clear as shining silver
rolling along the muddy path.
And there I sat
as two ducks were taking their noonday bath.
The fish swam and flipped.
Into the water, the thirsty bird dipped
his dry orange bill.
The cows were grazing on a distant hill
on fresh green clover.
Here I sat for endless hours
and now the day is almost over
because the sun of blazing fire
is sinking into golden fields
beyond the grass covered hill --

not to appear again till dawning,
and now I find myself yawning!
It has been a wonderful day!
I now start back the darkening way.
The birds are going into the trees.
The red and brown are now black leaves.
The old rooster all day running loose
is now going into the shed to roost.
Yes, the day is done,
but another will come
with beauty too
and I shall walk again
through the beautiful woods
and tread the hills of clover
a million times over
and observe that within
and beauty shall I find
but shall not see —
for I – am blind.

Black is Black
-1964-

The eyes of scorn survey my face
And shirk though touched by no disgrace.
The mouths curl up to yield a scowl
As though the nose smells something foul.

Though words of mine fall on their ear
They act as though they do not hear,
And when their eyes are cast on me
They frown and yet they do not see.

Oh, once I shook a friendly hand
But we were voters in demand;
And some put on the peaceful guise
When all they want's the Nobel Prize.

Deep down they want no part of me,
No justice, no equality.
They shake a different-colored hand;
They never look to see the man.

Some often speak of brotherhood
And meet their neighbors in the wood.
Their robes of white are far from pure
And bleeding is no more a cure.

Yes, he who hesitates must die
And he who thinks can't help but cry,
But men are these far more than they
Who waste the world in bloody fray.

Black is Black *(cont.)*

Perhaps, we'll compromise someday
When darker skies are lighter gray,
When hatred from the God of Hell
No longer in our hearts can dwell.

Right now the Christians drink their tea
And let me die in agony,
Outside their very window there
As if they do not even care.

Perhaps they don't .... how could I know?
If I asked them to tell me so,
Would they just smile and tell a lie
And force some superficial sigh?

Why are we different 'neath the sun:
The Jew, the Pole, the Mexican?
It is the same for all of us:
Somewhere our skin will make one cuss.

And he who curses in his might
Sees the darkness in the light,
All full of facts and yet no truth
He has a theory but no proof.

He thinks he's chosen by the Lord
And yet he is a mouse who's roared,
His bitter soul the devil bought;
His words are loud but they say naught.

Black is Black (cont.)

And with his twisted sight so dim
He drags more men down after him:
Some men who hate and know not why,
Who kill the truth to hide their lie.

I do not know why I was born
Into a life of hate and scorn,
Why I must be the last in line,
Why I must look for my own sign;

Why I must be a servile saint
And catch my brother if he faints,
And yet watch him break all the rules,
Spit in my face and call me fool;

Why I'm denied the schools to be
Condemned for my illiteracy;
Why I am labeled with gross sins
For just the color of my skin;

Why I am hung in effigy
And know of no serenity;
Why all the world knows less and less
Of understanding, happiness.

Perhaps someday we'll know no hate;
To live tomorrow is our fate,
And now we focus on today
For yesteryear has gone its way.

Black is Black (cont.)

The "right" we called in ages past
Today we know is "wrong" at last.
No, man should not rule man, it's true;
It is by God we are imbued.

But men must keep their petty fears,
Their dark suspicions through the years.
They must be loud, exalt themselves
And hide the mirror on the shelf.

So often I detect a face
And note a tear my mind can't trace,
See sadness that no words express,
See answers I can't hope to guess.

See eyes that know to look ahead,
See ears that should forget what's said,
See lips concealing deepest thoughts,
See wrinkles that are worry wrought,

See feet that have nowhere to walk,
A tongue that has no room to talk,
See only skin and not the man,
Someday, perhaps, ...someday we can.

But someday is a long, long time
When this day will be lost in rhyme,
In dusty books in musty rooms
That are forgotten in the gloom.

Black is Black (cont.)

So see we cannot now forget
Or else the crime stays with us yet.
We right it now once and for all;
Perhaps our children will not fall.

Their eyes may yet be opened wide,
Not dim like ours because we've cried,
Because we wince to feel our pain,
Because it's still the same again.

Oh, close my eyes and let me think
And let me of the darkness drink;
Maybe some solace I will find,
Maybe some comfort for my mind.

For after all he is like me:
His skin is black for all to see
And yet men do not curse the night
Or welcome it less than the light.

So why? But daybreak it shall come
And once again the face turns glum,
And answers that the night had shown
In morning light they are not known.

So I must be content to be
Pushed back by fameless majesty,
A false pretense with silent force,
A color that proclaims remorse.

But never, never knowing why,
No never, only...that... that I
Am black and for that should be sad,
Not knowing ever why it's bad.

Bldg. 110 Canteen (Hampton)
VA Medical Center Aug 2 '92

Sunday morning and no one to be found except a few smokers out front like they always are. The lobby was empty and no information booth. Antiquated display of medical paraphenalia under heavy glass; pictures on the wall, mismatched chairs. Dim ceiling light and only minimal light infused from the bright day outside. The basement. Bathroom with a latrine that wouldn't flush. The canteen. Vending machines and such. USA Today. A formica table/ seats. Orange, very stark, very hard. A lot of woes. Wives and mothers grappling coarse napkins hiding tears, sitting in these hard seats. Men lighting up cigarettes with fatal resolve, knowing that at this late date lung cancers are autonomous. Inhaling Camels and Benson and Hedges through their tracheostomy sites: breaking the boredom, ignoring death, blowing smoke in its face. These hard, lusterless seats, these impassionate stalls – we dare not look on their undersides. Wives not knowing how much of the problems are physical or mental. Men, jerked from the farm at 18 to fight a ruthless foe. Men scarred in their minds, their emotions, their bodies. Why is it that sometimes after you've been to Hell, everything looks and feels and smells like Hell for a long time?

Agony for their broken men. In these cushionless stalls. Nothing on the walls, not even "microwave in use"!

Sitting here while their husbands are fitted with prosthetic eyes and legs and penises. Fearing that there will never be cosmetic or functional improvement? How many are right?

Watching their husbands shrivel away with chemotherapy and cancer that prompted it. Yellow cadavers moving slowly, deliberately, haltingly toward the great exit. Not looking back. Passively accepting "help" without comment because they deserve it. Whatever can be done, they deserve it.

Sitting in this place and talking about their husbands, their plight, what is being done.

In these stark booths, at these hard tables. This is life like they've always known it: hard like these tables.

43

But Can We Feel Why?

It's easy to be complex.
It's easy to depress when we try to impress
and some form of regression always
accompanies progress.

We engineer our life-lies well
but still admit our emptiness.
We have a nice I'm-smiling-at-you-because-
you-smiled-at-me smile.
We even have a few quotes from Nietzsche
and Plato in our repertoire.

We can distinguish iambic pentameter
  from aldehyde
and probably Gainsborough from Camus.
We often have solutions before
  we can understand the problem,
And we can spot a hebephrenic a block away.

But can we feel why?

But Fly Not Near the Wood

Ah, wing above the heightened din
    of traffic in the street,
Of laughter and of solemn words,
    of trains and restless feet.
Amid the fog, the smoke, the smog,
    fly on, for it is good;
but fly not near the Wood, O fowl,
    fly not near the Wood.

Glide in and out the steepled towers,
    the frequent haunts of men.
The world below waits not for you
    nor cares where you have been.
But in the dark and evil Wood,
    the hunter holds his breath
and with his gun held tightly, waits
    for you, dear bird, your death.

So float above the busy town,
    beyond the fowler's eye
beyond enchanted groves of oak,
    beyond a clear blue sky.
O, be content to flit your wings
    where once tall trees have stood;
but fly not near the tranquil Wood —
    dear bird, not near the Wood.

Career Consciousness

I've told her so many disheartening things
I've chosen books over her
career over her
or at least on equal basis
when I know that love is the meaning of life
for God is love
and Love is God
He is in love
and in us
And the more love we have for others
the more real God is to us.
Why do we ever feel empty, helpless, useless?
Because we have abandoned the powers of love.
Free flowing love always comes back
if it doesn't find a receptor...
And to know that I have loved
brings me the greatest piece of mind.
I'm all caught up in the future
forfeiting the loves of the past
the opportunities of the present
you and God.

Carry Away the Old Man

Carry away the old man

For he is much too old.

Carry away the young man

For he is much too bold.

Take from here the prejudiced

For we've no use for them,

And take away the egotist

For we've no need of him.

Ask the radicals to leave

For they are out of place.

And tell the infidels to go

For they will cause disgrace.

Now the meeting has begun . . .

Hey! Where is everyone?

Come Hither Dear Democracy

Sail On! Sail on Democracy!
Sail o'er the swirling, troubled sea!
Sail on! We wait and watch for thee!
Sail on! Sail on, and make us free!

Bright lights are shining on the shore,
We hope shall burn forevermore.
So many ships have come before
But only you have we implored.

So sail on through the waters deep!
Sail on though waves around you leap!
For you the lighted lamp we keep;
Until you come we shall not sleep.

Sail on! Sail on! The port we fill.
Sail on! Sail on! For you we thrill.
Sail on! For you the bugles shrill.
Sail on! The lamp is lighted still.

Sail on! Sail on! ere you be late!
Sail on, ere darkness be our fate!
Sail on! Now all the people wait.
Sail on, and bring your priceless freight.

Sail on! Sail on! We wait for thee!
Sail on! Sail on and hear our plea!
Sail on, grand ship we long to see!
Sail on, O sweet Democracy!

Coming Home to You

There's a pale yellow moon
with gray on its face
in the west going down
and there's a golden sun
coming up in the east
above the sparkling ground
and I'm coming home to you
to your open arms
and I'm speeding down the silvery road.

And you sit and listen to the murmuring brook
and a cardinal comes for some grain
you have honey in tea
as you think of me
and suddenly it begins to rain
and I'm coming home to you
to your lovely smile
and now I'm only a few miles away
heading down that silvery highway.

I see your lovely visage so clear
I hear you whisper life in my ear
And now I'm just a few miles away
as I speed down that open highway.

There's a robin on the lawn pulling at a worm
as you wiggle your toes on the sidewalk
And you say a little prayer
that God'll get me there
And you smile cause you know
  we're gonna talk
and I'm coming home to you
to your open arms
and I'm speeding down the silvery highway.

49

Complementarity

Without your healing touch, your warmth,
I'm loose-ended, incomplete, unexpressed,
unfulfilled, hollow, superficial.

I *need* your smoothing closeness,
Your honest smile,
Your perceptive laugh
Your early morning gruffs,
Your nudity,
Your sensational nightdreams,
Your exciting daydreams,
Your love for simple things,
Your fear of bugs,
Your expressive toes,
Your quiet touch,
Your tolerance,
Your intense temper,
You ...
More time...
With you.

I love you.

David and Daniella

It was that time in life for a young man of eleven when he has renounced the feminine world, even to an extent of disowning the pampering life-giving breast of motherhood. It was a time when all recollections of "playing house" with sister had been conveniently repressed. And the once painful remembrance of playing nude with sister under the house, but a strange dream.

Being identical twins can bring a deal of accolade for one, and can interest the curiosity of others readily. There is security in the partnership and a good deal of promise that one will be dealt with justly. There is bargaining power and at the same time the possibility of mutual support. However, the case of fraternal filialship proves to be a completely different matter. Since the essential luxuries for males and females by nature, are different, protests of inequanimity are not uncommon. Then place the young male and female on the same birthday and the problem grows more acute.

Of course, another dilemma the prepubertal male must face is the growth rate of his fraternal sister. To the age of eight, he perpetuates the proverb of masculine strength with his elevated height. However, at about age ten he senses that his superior physical height is threatened by his blooming sister. It is at this time the male first resists the suggestion of female supremacy. At the same time, to make matters worse, he may have become acquainted with the statement that girls are smarter than boys. Such a blow to male ego most often results in a reaction syndrome in which he "humbugs" the feminine species, or otherwise he becomes feminine-minded himself, (if sees gain in the saying) that he might be reputed of intelligence.

Small wonders David often resented his sister, Daniella. Greater wonder that she maintained her respect and understanding. For Daniella, as we are to see, was a most unusual daughter and David, no less, a remarkable son.

David and Daniella *(cont.)*

Where their paths intersected remains a mystery, perhaps a good subject for hypnotic investigation or psychoanalysis, but at any rate a mystery. And though perhaps the etiology has been simulated before or after, the overt manifestations to my knowledge have been exceedingly rare.

Perhaps it was seeing Daniella cook, or sweep floors, or play the piano, or smiling in the summer breeze, which made David aware of a feeling somewhere inside of him. Furthermore, it is quite a surprising thing to suddenly, or even gradually, realize a reverse in one's feelings toward one previously the object of animosity. It was Daniella's integrity of personality, her consistency, her forgiving laugh of careless, untactful remarks, that won the soul of her associates. And though David began to realize the revival of his physical ascendance he was equally aware of his emotional subordination to his sister.

Soon David realized that the secret of Daniella's endorsement by her parents was simply that she deserved it. It is easy to blame luck, "hook and crook", and favoritism but at one time or another in our lives each of us must yield to the verisimilitude of another's nobility and superior quality. The realization often causes a dull pang in the stomach, an inexplicable melancholia, a degree of self abasement, and a desire to give up our seemingly petty and fruitless labors.

David became cognizant of the fact that he was all the same treated as a lovable son but not really as a maturing individual. It was in these discoveries that he was surged with the idea to do something outstanding and undeniably mature to impress his parents and build his new image. The problem was that David was bereft of ideas. Here again, David felt rather impotent: he was relatively unimaginative. At numerous times he thought of enlisting the service of his sister (Daniella) but dismissed the idea with internal violence each time.

David and Daniella *(cont.)*

At about this time, David questioned his striving and the real truth came. Was he just trying to gain his parents' approval and admiration? Was he bargaining for collusion of grown-up matters, or for gifts, or for more freedom, more responsibility, all of these?

Perhaps. But it became clear to David that his parents' praise was secondary to Daniella's; and it was her attention that he was trying to procure. In a manner, he was quietly crying out for equality, for love. The idea, in its small way, first appeared absurd to him and he strove unceasingly to mentally deny it. Perhaps, this mode of behavior served to reinforce the motive. For it is almost a truism that that which we fight so passionately is exactly the object of our passion.

Daniella remained constant to the unrefined overtures and pretensions of her brother save for a seldom condescending or instructive smile. David's heart burned more each day. At his wit's end, he finally decided to give in completely to his passion or deny it all together. However, love is similar to a seed in that no matter how long it is kept dormant, in sufficient conditions it will grow.

Then were the days of pretended detachment, coolness, even aloofness. The "If I can not be as good, I will be better" days. The self punishment was painful. Possibly, even in David's subconscious he wished Daniella to suffer because she had inspired in him what were surely forbidden thoughts. It is strange that men so quickly disembrace thoughts of love and perpetuate those of hate.

By degrees, David realized that he was envisioning an ideal woman whose personnage and countenance resembled too closely that of his sister. In fact, this fashioned subject became so foremost in his thoughts that at fifteen it was difficult for him to date like other boys of his age. It also seemed unnatural to him that he was possessed with jealousy when Daniella went on a date.

53

David and Daniella *(cont.)*

There was a feeling creeping over David from deep inside of him that received dubious welcome. It was a strong, intense emotion or feeling or whatever. Perhaps it breathed of hate, or fear, or love.

David experienced such a restlessness and irritability at this time that he feared it jeopardized his hard work for instatement. Yet, at the same time he felt rather inept to do much about it. He finally had to come to the confession: He loved Daniella. This seems the ideal in filial relationships. But, he *desired* her.

The frightening question foremost in David's mind was this: was such a feeling normal? Did all brothers experience this at some time for a sister? Was it a transient preoccupation or fleeting folly? However, David did not dare to find out by asking friends, or his parents, and least of all Daniella. Would she know anyway? Perhaps, she was more fallible than he thought. And possibly she wasn't due such exoneration. But, however David tried to demean his fixation, the irrevocable truth seared to his core: He loved her; but more, he desired her.

David had heard that he who looks on his mother's nakedness sins, and he thought "what more a sin to desire your sister." Although his parents could never have known, David found it hard to meet his father's eyes. He even found it more difficult to listen to his mother read the Bible. He seemed so unworthy to listen and blasphemous. After one such nightly perusal, Mrs. Carmichael inquired: "David is there something wrong? You've seemed unnaturally quiet, and your father and I have both noticed that you haven't eaten enough lately to keep a sparrow alive. Have we done something wrong? Have we failed to be good parents? I know young men are quite sensitive at this time in their development. Have we not been understanding enough...?"

At this point, tears came to David's eyes and he was ashamed of them.

54

David and Daniella *(cont.)*

"There, there," his mother affectionately responded as she drew him closely to her left breast. Her hands ran through his long blond hair. For a moment, David was again a four-year-old.

He had just stumped his toe and mother kissed it to make it well. He remembered crying just a little louder then so he would be drawn closer. Now it seemed that fewer tears were necessary. His impulse at last was to draw away for after all... but his mother held him closer still.

"David," his mother was speaking again, even more softly and comforting, "Daddy and I love you very, very much. We love both our children so very much. You are all we have. You are a part of us, and we can't bear to see either of you despondent. David, is there..." There was a pause as if she hesitated to say the next word, like a blind man who has undergone an operation to regain his sight and is fearful to remove the bandages that may or may not let in light. Then again she started the sentence: "Is there something you wish to tell me?"

The tears seemed to dry immediately in David's eyes. All of a sudden he felt betrayed, bemeaned, like love was conditional. He felt the dagger of the loving arm. He felt like Julius Caesar, or Judas, or Jesus, or anyone who has ever suffered tenderly. And yet he realized that his defensiveness only served to reinforce his mother's suspicion that something was indeed awry.

His mother stared at him silently, pensively, not harshly or insistent. It seemed like eternities of sorrow passed in those few short moments of solitude. A thousand responses entered David's mind; everything from the truth to "nothing", a lie. And since he felt that lying would be as incriminating as the truth, he remained silent — all except for his heart. It pounded like that of a much younger boy, he thought.

Soon he realized that his hand was yet inside his mother's and she squeezed it in a manner as if to say: "It's okay.

David and Daniella *(cont.)*

I understand." Then she stood up to her tall stature, only
bending once to kiss him on the cheek. Then David's mother
was gone, out of his room; and to him it seemed, out of his
life. Yet at the same time she had communicated to him a
thousand promises of trust, devotion, respect, and love in the
squeeze.

Yet, David knew one thing for sure: His mother surely did
not understand for her understanding of such an unthinkable
matter was, for the most part, unthinkable.

Soon the interrogation was forgotten, or at least David
reasoned that such a desire as his was beyond suspect. At
least he became less anxious about the feelings he could not
deny.

How the abrupt change occurred in David's logic is an
enigma. Perhaps, we can all find justification for our
daydreams, our imaginations, our secret desires. But the
fruition of such desires — ah, there is the difficult reconciliation.

At this time David had mounted the stage for his round of
applause, and was surely not unworthy of adulation. He was
the Adonis and knight of his group. He acquired the highest
marks of his class and not only was he intelligent but handsome. He was of perfect stature and his hair of blonde
coupled with his dark brows, grey eyes, and smooth skin,
made him an attractive sight for the girls his age and even
the older women.

David's mother once remarked if Mr. Carmichael had
been that debonair during their courting period, she would
have never married him. This seemed strange to David and
he pursued the conversation of his mother, who seemed to be
waiting for someone to ask the reasoning.

"When people are pretty they are often told that. They
come to believe it, if they did not already. This is all right

David and Daniella *(cont.)*

unless the person begins to worship his beauty as his salvation rather than relying on his intellect, will, or empathy.
What would a person then revert to in old age? There are
two types who spend too much time at a mirror: The pretty
who constantly are viewing themselves to see if they've lost
any beauty; and the ugly who constantly seek to gain pretti-
ness. But, of course, my son you have more than initially
meets the eye and therefore you may capitalize on your looks
as an additive and not as the case in point."

It was certainly a living truth that David had and was
succeeding. His athletic prowess gained him much admiration from those mobs of devoted men who enjoy vicarious
sublimation in their sons' shoes. David was also highly
regarded by the ladies as "a gentleman in all his words and
deed."

Such developments brought quite a deal of joy to Mr. &
Mrs. Carmichael; but this was only half the joy. Daniella had
established herself as quite an artist in the community and
everyone peddled their poster boards to her for inscription
(although she did not relish such forms of art). At first she
had dabbled with landscapes, watercolors, and the usual one,
two, threes of art. Then Daniella took to abstract art, pictures
of great beauty of little expression to the common viewer.
She entered several in art shows on different occasions and
was disappointed and even dismayed that such creations
habitually won. At last Daniella turned to the form of art she
felt held the greatest challenge for her artistic ability: Realistic portraiture with impressionistic undertones.

At times she was assailed by a face in her mind, a haunting countenance that persisted until she had completed the
final stroke of the painting. At other times she would be
"filled with colors" in her mind of such magnificence she was
unable to express. When she painted, Daniella injected all
her powers of heart, and soul, and mind into her work.

David and Daniella (cont.)

And her creations reflected her labor. For she was not just a painter, but an artist.

Once when Daniella confessed to her mother the unusual way she received inspiration, Mrs. Carmichael was frightened. And, of course, I guess it would seem strange to most anyone who envisions the stereotypical painter sitting his easel on the banks of the Seine to paint the tawny sunscape. The fact was that Mrs. Carmichael felt there were more worthwhile diversions and occupations for her daughter. She never actually scolded Daniella's hobby outright but she incessantly dropped little implications that showed her indifference. She would point out some domestic accomplishment of one of Daniella's friends and add, "What a wonderful wife she will make," or "She is certainly a mature young woman." And in her subtle or perhaps subconsciously-dictated manner, Mrs. Carmichael found the way to really hurt a human being: Demean the thing they hold most dear. As a result, their relationship was (not apparently but under the surface) strained. And Daniella felt that if her mother could not accept this vital and most important aspect of her being, she would rather all of it were rejected.

Of course, Mrs. Carmichael was not aware of her daughter's resolution and Daniella gave her no reason to suspect it, in that she did not resort to pouting, indifference, or flagrant cries and tantrums for justice. She was a well ordered child and she smiled her tears away admirably.

Daniella's hair was now long as a winter's night, blond and beautiful. She was a blond but unlike whatever blonds are supposed to be. She road a horse well but it was not her equestrian skill that made the men feel awed but her great knowledge about the needs of such animals for humane treatment. She once remarked laughingly that the man who reciprocated as much love as her horse would certainly be

58

her choice. In fact this might have been one of the distin-
guishing features of David's sister: her humane treatment of
others. She was not one to jeer, gossip, or betray her
feelings. She was honest with herself and somehow inspired others to follow suit. I suppose she felt that man was
inherently good and, if each man communed with his inner
edicts and acted accordingly, each man would do good for
his fellow. This was Daniella's charisma.

At 17, David was the game of all the gals. It seemed that
each of them had engineered plans whereby they might gain
his favor. If they weren't so ingenious they took to day-
dreaming, waiting for that golden moment when he would
ask them to be his. One girl even had a school yearbook so
rigged that if anyone should open it the predominant picture
viewed would be that of David, coincidentally, "my future
husband."

However, David kept the true course as one might say in
that he did not rely dependently on his physical endow-
ments but avidly pursued the development of his mental
powers and social skills. Mrs. Carmichael once remarked
that he "would just love them and leave them." And she
seemed quite happy about it for mothers hate to lose sons as
much as fathers do daughters.

It was about at this time that once again David reviewed
his latent desire for his sister. The fire had never died. The
coals had just been hidden, pushed back into the crevices
men dig for their mistakes. But inevitably one must
stumble onto them again in treading through the past.

And the thought could have been as hot as a glowing
coal as David handled it haltingly but curiously. He had
wished that the fire would be quenched completely; that he
could grasp it as an outworn invention or a spool of thread,
but not so. As soon as his mind once again focused on his
inner feelings he came to realize that he had never felt

David and Daniella *(cont.)*

otherwise since the earliest time of his realization. The
result was a comingling of passive acceptance and hopeless
incidence.

"Can a man live outside his desires? Is it necessary that
he do so? If a man feels something so strongly he can hardly
contain it, should he not express it in some way?" The
questions ran through David's mind. He thought, perhaps,
that he had fashioned an ideal, with Daniella the model. And
why shouldn't a brother think highly of his sister? This was
the young woman with whom he had been associated for
the longest. Yet, no matter how he tried, David could not
justify or explain his love for his sister on the normal
grounds of fraternity. No, there was more, much more.

. . . .

It is quite imaginable to realize the amount of introspection,
retrospection, and anticipation which ensued thereafter.
David's head became tender with thought and yet passions
perpetuate the man; prepare him, and give him pretense.

The foremost questions in David's mind were these:
should he unequivocally decide that he desired Daniella as a
lover, should he tell her? If so, how would he go about it?
When Daniella learned how would she react?

"Of course, the Bible teaches against incest... but I'm not
thinking of incest! Or am I? Could I be? What have I
become? What am I? I'm obsessed!"

It's so easy to do nothing. Winter days are conducive to
such inactivity. You can put your nose against a frosted pane
and rationalize away a thousand duties. Each day only gave
more credence to David's fear, and soon his dreams were of
the most restricted sort. The female was always Daniella.

Once he dreamed that he and Daniella were together in
bed and were discovered by their mother. She only

remarked, " you are both blonds. It isn't right." Another
time he dreamed that his father was after him with a hatchet
because Mr. Carmichael desired Daniella and wanted her
for himself. To David, the dreams all seemed inconsequen-
tial, enigmatic, and as natural as the next person's but —
they were not easily forgotten.

It was a December morning, Saturday morning. It gave
every promise of a bleak day.

When David awoke Mrs. Carmichael had bacon cooking
and the smell seemed to fill the house with its capability to
inspire hunger. The brewing coffee emitted an aroma which
seemed to smooth troubles even better than clean, warm
sheets.

David struggled out of bed and almost retreated back in
when his feet hit the cold floor. He managed a pair of
pants, his wool flannel shirt, and his leather shoes, without
socks.

The fires had been extinguished at bed time and each
time he breathed through his mouth, the air filled with icy
vapor.

As David passed through the living room on his way to
the kitchen he regarded the old piano. His mother had
refinished it but for some reason had never had it retuned.
He imagined how the notes might feel on such a cold
morning. At least they had an excuse — but no one would
probably know otherwise.

The plastic curtain covering the french doors into the
kitchen was torn at the handle and David mused momentarily if it were not the result of someone's haste to get to a
warmer place.

The kitchen was so warm. It's kind of like a cold
shower, or sudden tears. It really goes to the bone, David
thought, and it felt good.

David and Daniella *(cont.)*

His mother, with one hand on the skillet handle and the other
with the spatula, performed her perfunctory early morning
forehead kiss. David realized how bad his breath might be.
He sat down in the white wooden chair in front of the
stove. It was the one his dad sat in each morning so it was
warm already. Dad had already been up hours and gone to
his carpentry. David pulled off his shoes using his feet,
scooted his chair back, and then felt the warming sensation
as he propped his bare feet close to the fire. In fact, he was
sure if at any time he had held his feet in a position 10
seconds longer they would have been seared. The meal of
breakfast was delicious. Eggs, bacon, buttered biscuits, and
blackberry jam were, it seemed to David, a fitting elixir to
any of man's needs. Halfway through the course of David's
breakfast, Mrs. Carmichael announced that it was necessary
she walk downtown to the store to secure some tasties for
Sunday dinner since the pastor was coming over. David
reflected that if he were a preacher, and could get by with it,
he would eagerly do the same. For a moment he felt superior
to his mother in that she seemed to put divine significance on
the event whereas he felt it a filching.
   Suddenly a thought hit him: "Well what about
Daniella?" He hadn't really meant to say it but the sudden
concern was so strong that he blurted out..
   "Well," his mother queried in a trailing voice, "What
about Daniella?" David was not one to inspire thoughts or
imaginations in channels in which he felt might bring him
discredit, so he quickly assumed a quieter discipline and
asked in an almost indifferent tone:
   "What about her breakfast."
   "Well indeed," replied his mother assuming a gentle
countenance, "She must be at the church this morning at ten-
thirty for the cantata rehearsal. I can understand why the
poor dear is still under covers. She went sleigh riding last
night out at the Beckmans and that cold wind is enough to
make anything hibernate."

David and Daniella (cont.)

David glanced at the clock: ten past nine. "I'll fix her breakfast", he beamed. "That will help her get ready more quickly!"

The idea went over well with Mrs. Carmichael. In fact, she was almost overwhelmed by David's enthusiasm. And he felt trusted.

He held his breath almost as she left the kitchen to get her coat. He didn't know whether she would go by Daniella's room to wake her. He hoped not. She didn't. And he was so ecstatic because he not only had an opportunity to cook Daniella breakfast but to wake her. He had a chance to be close to her.

Then many things flashed through David's mind. His heart beat faster. His stomach felt full of butterflies instead of biscuits and bacon. He thought of slipping into her room and kissing her awake and explaining it as a joke. Or he thought of pulling back the cover to touch her breast — but he was afraid she would awake. Then he was in a quandary: should he go wake her now and cook her breakfast while she was getting dressed or should he cook the food now and then wake her? But by then she would already be awake and dressed. Which would she appreciate more? Which would bear him the greatest chance to look at her.

It felt like a thousand wild horses inside of him. He was afraid his heartbeat would wake her and he so much wanted to do it with a touch, a closeness.

His hand reached the knob on her door and he expected it would be cold inside. His heart took a giant step as he quietly opened the bedroom door and stepped in. The first thing he noticed was that it was warm in the room though not quite as warm as the kitchen. The bathroom door had been left open and the undulating warmth pulsed to even the corner of the room.

David dared not scare his sister since this was the only time he could remember waking her since she developed

David and Daniella *(cont.)*

breasts. If she happened to awake and saw a man, or even if she thought it him she might be frightened.

So David tiptoed to the window and raised the shade. The day wasn't much to speak of and he felt sorry for the sparrows clinging to the frozen branches of an humbled tree. The dismal light illuminated the small room and then David saw.

At first he wanted to run, run, run. To live in a world of broken dreams. To escape reality. What he saw was not a horrible sight but a most beautiful one. The kind of thing that makes most of us feel a deep sense of inadequacy for we are not all creators and we definitely fear that which we cannot understand. But, a horrible act, we rarely run from, for it reflects the side of us we all know too well.

Daniella was lying half on her right side and half on her stomach. Her right arm was drawn under her and her right hand close to her face. She had pulled the cover down and it revealed the smallest hint of the separation of her hips. Her back seemed the prize of an ivory craftsman and her slender arms embraced rest like a lover.

Deep in David's mind was an ominous feeling. At any moment he felt his mother might return, or Daniella might awake. But at the same time he was so fascinated by Daniella's beauty that he could not move in any direction. He felt like an explorer discovering an ancient tribe who views them from a distance for fear of capture.

David had been holding his breath almost the entire time. Now moving his station to the left of the foot board he could see her breast. Milky white, smooth as rivers make stones. For David, the desire to hold one of Daniella's breasts in his hands was overwhelming. Yet at any second he feared she might awake and he would have quite a bit of difficulty explaining his unannounced presence.

David and Daniella (*cont.*)

He wanted to touch her back, some part of her for memory, but he knew she would awake. So he looked at least for a time more and gently covered his desire with grandmother's quilts. Then he kissed her head ever so gently and retreated toward the door. Opening the door, he began knocking on it and said: "Daniella, sweet sister, wake up! How can your love find you if you are still in bed. Wake up! Sweet, sweet sister. The church needs your voice, Mother needs your hands, and I need your smile. Wake up!"

· · · · · · ·

Dear Baptist Bookstore

Dear Baptist Book Store:

Just to inform you that I am no longer church librarian, you can terminate my subscription to the weekly catalog. Also you can terminate the church's materials for awhile. The church burned to hell yesterday. The fire started in the library.

Yours entirely.

Death of a Tree

They creak, they groan
They cry, they moan
As they're cut down
As they crack and fall to the ground
As they die, never to rise again
above the valley below, hidden within its shadow
in summer (never to reach toward the sky)
And arched by its arms in winter, Heavenly lofts
(for daring birds) are crushed beneath the foot of man.

Though nature has won its share of the battles,
Man is winning the war at present.
Grind and rip and saw and cut this elegant edifice
into a geometric conformity for man's use.
It's hard to know how it can give more pleasure–
As it was or will be, though I tend to think the former.
The periphery of my forest Shangri-La is no longer majestic.
Large stumps signify those who have gone on to the dictates
of man, the constructor — and destroyer.

Small trees try to hide the gap by stretching their branches,
and use rationale such as "this will give us more room to grow."
But they know, Man will come again in a hundred years
or two hundred years, he will come again —
and they will not survive the slaughter.

Near Fordyce, Arkansas

67

Deja-Vu

I am convinced we met before
      on a foggy day
you were there and I was there
It was a time we knew
It was a feeling we could touch
and a look we could hear
And now you're given to lesser preoccupations
so that your looks are reserved
      for the select,
your thighs for the elect
and your feelings for neglect.

Delta Despondence

Sometimes when I'm lonely for you
I think of summer:
- the oppressive heat generated by a distant billow
  of black smoke;
- the disturbing harshness of sunshine and steam after a
  refreshing downpour
- an aborted thunderstorm
- a sticky hot highway with no car in sight
- the repugnant odor of trash burning in the open barrel
- the parched grass; the cracked soil; the brown leaf
- the dry stream
- the incessant rays of sun
- the sweat; the grime
- the brassy smell
- the sunburn
- the death shuffle of dry cottonwood leaves
- the panting, drenched dog
- the stuffy car
- the moan of mowers on a Sunday morn
- the relentless weeds and strangling vines
- the endless, timeless stretches of light
- the ennui of lapping waves on the open lake
- the premise, the promise, the guise of
  but a temporary chaos
- the itch in the creases
- the kamikaze scream of insects
- the lament of the powerless young bird prematurely
  prodded from the nest
- the fires, the squints, the sirens, the license, the ruin

Departure

we smile as much as we can
remembering soon that we must frown
the birds are busy with their nests
the last trees are turning green
I look down and kick a stone into the pond
and we both watch as ripples circle out
to our imaginations
subsiding at last to truth
you turn your face away to hide your
tears from me
but I know
for I am crying too

La Push, Washington

70

Departure

A word and I leave you
      To go, you to stay
For now it is night and
      Tomorrow is day.

I'm leaving this evening
      For you all well know
If morning I waited
      I'd probably not go.

Depression

Things down here are pretty sad
since you are not here,
and though I left you days ago
It now seems like a year.

A year or so of loneliness
That calls the fervor done
Like roses caught by late spring frost
or snowflakes by the sun.

Like maples with no hope of spring
Or bees of flowers sweet
Like sparrows with no songs to sing
Or farmers fields of wheat.

Like idle hours remembered when
Our failings meet our eyes
Like many lives (we think) we'd love to live
When we must stop to die.

Like tawny sunsets slipped away
Forever growing cold
Like endless tickings of a clock
That say we must grow old.

Like water dripping from the tap
Within an empty room
Like shadows of another day
That bear a faint perfume.

Depression (cont.)

Like empty words on deafened ears
Or kisses on cold lips
Like dreams that never can come true
Or tactless words that slip.

Like years, eternities of night;
No greeting at the door
Like tears upon a wrinkled face
Yes, all of this and more.

Die, Die, Die My Heart

Die, die, die my heart:
Give me no more your sentiments;
Your foolish cares, your sad events;
Die, die, die my heart.

Die, die, die my heart:
Goodbye to tears, they cloud my eyes;
Goodbye to laughter, child of lies;
Goodbye to love, it always flies;
And die, die, die my heart.

I leave no lantern at the door;
Nothing can hurt me anymore.
I now can hide the smile I wore
Forgetting that I ever smiled,
I ever smiled before.

Summer of mercy, Wichita, Kansas

Digressions of a Hollow Man
by Ken Helton

If Isabella sent Columbus

To sail across my soul

Would he discover virgin lands

Yielding spice and gold

Or would his three inquiring ships

Sail off into a void

And find behind my troubled heart

The far edge of the world

Disappointment

The world had slept away its fears
The gentle night had dried the tears
And all awoke to see new hope:
The sun would soon appear.

But leaden clouds obscured the day
The city wore a cloak of grey.
With all their sins remembered then,
They sadly went their way.

All those things which cause regret
They had ignored, tried to forget;
But sorrow does not fade away —
It is remembered yet.

Don't Question Why

Don't question why it must be done
The question has been asked before
But no one waits with a reply
For no one answers anymore.

Men only do what others do
Repeating words that others say
And, should you question, you will hear:
"No reason, this is just the way."

Don't Say Good-bye

Now when our love has tired so sweetly
And you must needs be on your way,
I ask of you one thing in parting:
Don't say "Good-bye"; just say "Good day."

True, every summer has an autumn
But winter, too, must have its spring
And so I beg, be kind in parting
For we've no mind to future things.

And when you kiss me last and tender
And hold me not so long and tight,
I pray one thing, oh may you hear me:
Don't say "Good-bye" just say "Good night."

For even if the sun be setting
We know the night must yield to morn.
And so is love: so often changing
But ever growing once it's born.

And so when you look back in leaving
I will not tell you not to cry
But at the gate so quietly ling'ring
I'll only say, "Don't say 'good-bye'."

Dr. Kinlaw's Suicide

Silence. Now it must be done.
Disbelief. And several rush in.
Shock. Someone picks up the gun.
Confusion. Is it a sin?

Stunned: Eyes meet eyes unwilling.
Sadness: The sound of women crying.
News: Outside a crowd is milling.
Inside: How could we know he was dying?

Dr. Turney's Office
Sept. 89

Being an internist I always flagellate myself
(probably unduly) about any bad outcome. Being a
Southern Baptist makes it doubly hard because I
constantly feel I have failed scientifically *and* spiritually. This type of dissatisfaction and self-defamation
is inspirational/motivational and constructive up to a
point. However, excessive goals sometimes postpone
all relaxation and allow no self-contentment or even a
deep breath or a few days between completing a
successful challenge and tackling a new one. In fact,
juggling three or four demanding tasks at the same
time may be usual.

The clarion call for achievement rises above the
adolescent milieu of mediocrity. It becomes difficult
to distinguish overachievement from a perception of
substandard gifts and underachievement.

Usual relationships pale in importance compared
to the charge for more papers, patients, procedures,
publications, professional pursuits. When and if
rejection occurs at the professional level, the usual
web of loving family and friendship support may be
tattered and torn. You eventually realize you are in a
real-life triathlon; competing against yourself and
that the competition is often unfriendly and
unhealthy.

Dusk

Serenely speaks the voice of dusk
to all her latticed children.
Silent songs with muted shades
of amber and vermilion.
Words so sweet that birds are hushed
And even the breeze is awed
For it moves not the sleepy trees
which loom as lifeless shadows.

Mt. Washington Hotel, New Hampshire

Each Case is Unique

And everywhere that Hans could look
Nadine could see much farther
The why, and if, and but of it
they never seemed to question.
Until the morn (it rained 'til night)
that caused them to look closer
And then the dark gave out its secrets
to all the hidden corners.
And then Hans' eyes were blind to all
Nadine could see less too
And though they never answered why —
they knew.

Early Feelings Rise to Memory

Early feelings rise to memory,
then are repressed by present implosions,
pieces of my prided ego
flung to my ear canals.
Shouting, stomping.
I have the floor;
you, the control.

Eavesdropping

The flowers have ears, you know,
and that is no disgrace.
One must have heard of my troubles;
there were tears all over her face.

Ephemeral

Time is fleeting, fleeting, fleeting
Nothing ever worth repeating
A wealth of pain and tears and bleeding
    Nothing more
And my name it is erasing
All my works of art effacing
Quickly covering and replacing
    all that's gone before.

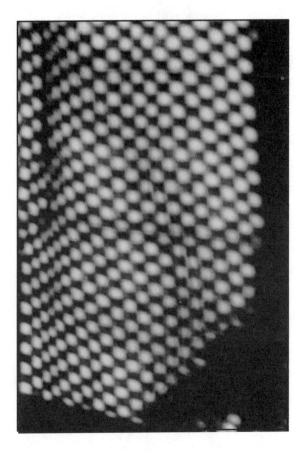

Fair are the Red Roses

Fair are the red roses
With dew on their face
Those tears at the morning
the sunshine doth trace
And I like the roses
who open in May,
Am sad, for my lassie
Has gone on her way.

She said "It is springtime
and still you carouse.
I'm leaving this heartbreak,
I'm leaving this house.
But when the red roses
Are sparkling with dew,
You'll know that I'm crying
And that I love you."

How red are the roses!
As red as my heart
The wound never closes
Those thorns do impart.
I try to forget her
but wherever I go
On hill or in valley,
the red roses grow.

Her presence was springtime
And fresh as the rain
That image of beauty
I know shall not wane
And after the roses
have wilted and gone
The thought of my lassie
shall live on and on.

Fair Winds

Ah yes, fair winds shall blow again
And fairer still shall blow;
And home I'll ride these cooling winds
O'er mountains capped with snow.

I'll take my berth inside her wings
And sweep o'er vales below
I'll fly with majesty of kings
So gracefully and slow.

Ah this one thing I do this day
Tomorrow may not come.
This breeze I take and go my way
And listen to her hum
She gives to me a drum to play
'til silent others come.

Asheville, North Carolina

Far, far beyond the call of conformity I rest
Beyond the alarms, the norms, the modes, the tests.

Farewell to Comrades

Farewell to thee, my comrades laughing,
Farewell to thee, my comrades free.
Though we may never meet again,
"Comrades" always let it be.

Let us leave and take our memories—
Memories of the conflict sore.
Cherish all the joy and sorrow—
Cherish, comrades, evermore.

Comrades, comrades, yes forever;
Here's a toast to all of ye.
As great kings or lowly beggars,
"Comrades" now and e'er to be.

Farewell to the Teacher
to Dr. John Douglas

He stood between me and the masses,
  guiding my hands to a better perception of the truth;
  alerting my ears to distant rumblings and murmurings,
  signifying ill-fated destinies;
  training my eyes to observe the obvious
  and to unveil the concealed.
He taught me questions and answers
  and answers to questions -
  and questions to answers.
He could chase the rabbit all day or whistle it to a stop.
He could be pertinent, cogent, masterful, expedient,
  pragmatic, definite, convicted, empathetic.
  And he could be satisfied.
He could transcend temporal laws with plausible
  progressions of conjectured events.
He was credible, honest.
He taught me to listen:
  courteously, quietly, patiently, expectantly,
  compassionately.
He taught me to note:
  the tone, the thrust, the covert tear,
  the worried stare, the despondent smile,
  the fisted salutation.
He taught me humility.
He taught me to lay on hands, to confer hope;
  selflessness.
He could look across the years with a downward glance -
  integrating scientific principles, human nature,
  intuition - pronouncing an outcome.
He could be proponent, opponent, advocate, declamant,
  captain, charge, companion.
He could be silent.

Farewell to the Teacher (cont.)

He could extract lessons from a twisted, terminal life form;
yet he exhibited respect for the unhearing, the unseeing,
the unknowing.
He could feel sorrow and joy and pain and love - and
death.
He could let a life slip through his fingers -
intellectually, philosophically, emotionally.
He could appreciate life outside the foggy windows,
above the gravel roof, beyond the haunting moans.
He could transmit the warmth of May sunshine, the
refreshing breath of autumn coolness, the solace of
a soft October rainfall.
He could be defeated. He could admit defeat. He could
rise again.
He could dream and plan and wrestle the future. He could
forget and remember the past. He could live by the
minute, the hour, the sundowns.
He could look beyond the transience and artificiality
of man-made deadlines, trivialities, limitations,
dogmas, reservations, to a divine order of principles,
encompassing time and life.
He could discover the motif, the integral thread,
the common link.
He could observe: obverse and reverse, antegrade and
retrograde, egression and accession, ascension and
descension. He found some sidewalks going to
burned houses.
He was not threatened by silence, frowns, laughter,
affection, rejection, inattentiveness, intensity,
awkwardness.
He could encourage with a challenging look, a firm touch,
a wager.
A serious student, soft-spoken skeptic, stolid supporter.

Farewell to the Teacher *(cont.)*

The farmer walked across the expansive field.
Fresh rain, black mud, warm earth;
no crop in sight.
Absent.
Seed? No.
Additions? No.
Conditions? No.
What?

> Too many crops in the farmer's field,
> Twice around, thrice around, four times
> to yield;
> Needs rest, input before it's tilled:
> Too many crops in the farmer's field.
> Too many crops in the farmer's field.

Off to the rainbow; then
  to the stars
the smell of old books and
  the rattle of jars.
Far from the ignorance
  of impassioned minds
  the scrutiny
  the thanklessness
  the reasons, the binds.
Alone self-dependent
  with room for retreat
unqualified rules
  no cause for defeat.

Farewell to the Teacher *(cont.)*

The crunch of brown leaves brought it all back.
The immobile rotting log, the brambles,
   the dry creekbed.
It had been so long since I had wiggled my toes.
I couldn't see them. The leaves crackled
to powder in my hands.
An appropriate stick served to find
a black beetle. With the smell of dust
in my nostrils I listened to the song of
a warbler.
It was worth this moment.
Case in hand, hand on the switch,
he stood in the doorway, the empty silence.
Tangential light exposed the greying head
and the wrinkled eyes.
Down the hall, oblivious laughter
trailed departing footsteps.
   A twitch of the mouth and closed eyelids,
a downward stare,
a tap of the foot in the doorway,
chin elevation,
brief shrug of the shoulders,
a sigh,
a fast over-the-shoulder look,
a tear,
darkness,
slam.
He was a friend.

Permission for use was granted by Alpha Omega Alpha Honor
Medical Society. Copyright, 1979.

First Poem

Coupeville, Washington   Geoff Bowles

I went to school today
And boy how good I play.

Fond Recollections
by Ken Helton

I have a tree inside my yard
(It isn't my yard at all,
Because for it my father
Mortgaged by mother's basketball)

This tree is often very brown
(Except whene'er it's green)
And roots which grow upon the limbs
Are almost never seen

Alas! Poor tree when it died
It never lived again
In sorrow deep I think of it,
And often crack a grin

For a Humane World

I lie in the cold, awaiting the sun,
In the frank darkness of despair.
And in my eye there waits a tear
That lets me know man still can care.

And on my face a question "why?"
But yet my lips are stricken dumb.
And though the sun may love me still
Today he will not come.

For see, they've pushed the button.

For Those Who Try to Keep Up With the Joneses

The sun was setting in the west,
The moon was swiftly rising,
Into the streets of this proud town
There came a slight surprising:
A runner from the land of Gaul
Did run and he was naked.
The women screamed, the men did blush,
And all the town was quaked.
Yet he did run without alarm
And all the men ran after.
The streets were filled with young and old
And all the town with laughter.
They ran on far into the night
And yet he did not flounder.
These men were all of high esteem
And no minds were the sounder
But when the morning light appeared
And all the men were tired, sir,
The Gauls surprised and slew them all.
The town destroyed in fire, sir.
The moral to this story now
Is told by the forsaken
Through acts to trap one may be trapped
And him and his be taken.

Friendship

I give to you a gift that's rare
And priceless as a precious stone.
A gift that you might not expect
Until your hopes are all but gone.
Just carry it next to your heart,
No matter where you plan to go,
And when you're blue and all is dark
Unwrap it then and watch it glow.
I give this present from my heart—
Now think it not so very strange.
For what nobler thing is there
Than blessed friendship to exchange?

From Vietnam - Dec. 1965

My Christmas tree
Is full of lights
They shine out through
The blackened night.
    They say they do
        I know they do
           and so it must be true.

They say there's snow
Upon the yard
And all the creeks
Are frozen hard.
    If I could see
        My Christmas tree
           How happy I would be.

But here the grass
Is emerald green
And snow it never
Has been seen.
    So fade sweet thought
        With comfort fraught
           This day peace must be bought.

Funeral

Everyone has touched the flowers
        to see him.
And some cry, and all sigh
(and Mrs. Apple thinks of her roast)
And they bring God into the situation
"It was God's will..."
and even though it may have been,
it makes the killer laugh

And someone saw a sunrise
And once I felt a sunset
I knew it wasn't true
so I forgave God.
And I forgot the face, the words,
the deeds
        The man who died
        The man who killed
And even how the flowers felt.

Futile Times

The calendar stares me in the face
along with the many unanswered letters
and unquestioned replies.
My pen is low on ink so I
don't start one if I can't start all
so I don't start any.
The story is too long to tell.
I see a man in the cracked mirror
or do I see in the mirror
a cracked man?

I wonder. But seldom.
I seldom wonder.
Mostly I just sit and think about
things I never did because I
never thought about doing them when
I could have done them.

I was never young
at least I don't ever remember being.
I've always been thinking about death.
So much I never took the time to live
for fear I'd die.
And that's exactly what I've been doing.
I tore all the months off that calendar
twenty years ago.
But it's okay,
Tomorrow is only yesterday again.

George, are you going to eat your broccoli?
(what about your potatoes?)

"And Dad, he has red meat every night. He'll have a whole plate of steak. Plus all kinds of other food on the side."
"Dad, he's gonna be one of your patients."
"You can tell he eats a lot of meat."
"How?"
"By the way he looks."
"Does he look *carnivorous*?"
"No, Dad, gross. He just looks puffy all in his face."
"And that's how you tell?"
"Yeah."
"OK."

I thought maybe he had mechanical stainless steel teeth and black eyes with bloodshot conjunctivae and eyebrows that grow together in the middle (I guess because my dad said you couldn't trust people with eyebrows like that).

You know, one of those guys that nibble on the raw hamburger meat while they're frying the patty.

Guys for whom the taste of blood is as natural and appealing as apricot nectar. These were the guys who sucked their blood when they cut themselves. People who think nothing of a big vein flopping out of their chicken leg or filet mignon. Meanwhile, I'm not only grossed out but I'm trying to remember its anatomical name.

I remember how grossed the girls were one time when a friend took us to Chateau Briand and ordered a steak rare. When he cut the meat and blood oozed out, they gasped.

We talked about the "G" word and all got instantly grossed out. You know, gristle.

Beef is "real food for real people" and, of course, pork promos are getting stronger. Fish with EPA, of course, can reduce heart attacks and prolong life. So meat's here to stay. "Eat no meat that has a face" is clever. However, the breed who can inhale a whole plate of ribs in five minutes is alive and well.

Shoot, let's keep those cholesterols up and keep those cards and letters (patients) rolling in.

When the 7-11 starts putting broccoli at the front counter instead of beef jerky, we'll know we've arrived.

Mustard Greens, Arkansas City, Arkansas

Gimme a Grant, Quick!

If I could find a reason for the whole mess
I would gladly say ok... here it is
get the ladle out and lap it up,
gulp it down,
regurgitate, urinate, defecate, reciprocate
and should you computerize
the same answer as mine
we would both win a trip to
Inner Latvia
as government advisers on the grain beetle problem
And we would inspect the wheat every morning
from 11:30-12:00,
win the nobel prize, and get rich on government
allocations.
Get drunk, go naked,
and die at the age of 96
without ever seeing one of those
damn beetles.

Give Me Flowers While I'm Living

I have ridden on the condor
in a raging hurricane.
I have swum the deepest ocean,
run along the fastest train;
but there's no thrill so great as friendship
when the tinsel's turned to dust
and the yoke that firmly links us
is an iron that will not rust.

(So) give me flowers while I'm living
Give me love while I can see
There'll be time enough for crying
There'll be tears enough for me.

I was once trapped in a valley
by the thorns of my own sin.
I was smothered, drowning, sinking
with no hopes to rise again.
But Jesus came and took my burden;
rubbed the pumice in my wounds.
He the great and morning star
created me and sun and moon.

(So) give him prayers while you're living
Give him love while you still live.
Time will come when you are dying
(When) just the soul is left to give.

Give Me Flowers While I'm Living (cont.)

I was standing on a mountain
looking out across the sea;
a thunderhead so grey and mighty
reached up to eternity.
Stars and comets, moons and planets
turned their faces to the light
of the holy Son of God
coming down in glory bright.

There was rain on my eyelashes...
or were they tears? I could not tell.
I felt love and joy and sorrow,
blissful heights and darkened hell.
There were huddled masses screaming;
trampling, crying for reprieve
but Gabriel had closed the volume:
"These we take; no more believe."

(So) give me flowers while I'm living
Give me love while I can see
There'll be time enough for crying
There'll be tears enough for me.

Give Me the Moon

I love the moon, the moon loves me
In a lagoon or on the sea
You may prefer fun in the sun
but winter or June
Give me the moon.

I love the moon, the moon loves me
It's so serene, tranquility
You may believe I'll change my tune
but young or old
Give me the moon.

Give me the moon
you take the sun
and I'll take moonbeams
    for everyone.

107

God and premarital sexual intercourse

God forgive us if we made our love too soon
if we surrendered to our secret desires,
but God we have
and I am so happy we have.
But God though my mind is content
my body is hungry, my body cries for her
I ache for her, I love her God
and there is no way for us to live apart.
Once inside her soul I want to stay and it is
not the fact of being there but
staying there which brings the fear.
It is like the sirens, Lord.
Oh God why must we wait? Why do we wait?
I pray thee God take away this burning need,
or let me quench my thirst
or let me die.
Inside of her we are so close and
all the other times we feel as if we
can't get close enough.
God can you be too close?
God she hurts for me,
we hurt for each other,
the world hurts for us.
God how bad did you hurt when Jesus hurt?

God is Dead

God is dead. He never lived.

It took no god to make the earth,
The sea, the sky, the universe
That fits together in a plan
That still no man can understand.

It took no god to make a tree,
The beasts, the fish within the sea.
And human beings just evolved.
Oh yes, the world is well nigh solved.

I'm sure they'll make a man quite soon
Or maybe they'll adjust the moon.
It took no god to do these things
And man can fly and have no wings.

And birth I'm sure quite soon it will
Be that our children come from pills,
For there's no miracle in birth;
That's mighty plain throughout the earth.

It took no god up high above
To make me see two people love
And walk to church now hand in hand---
God's dead! Why can't they understand?

There is no god who gave me breath
When I was on the bed of death.
(Twelve times --- I nearly died the twelfth!)
Where was a god who could have helped?

No god. No god. No, god is dead.
Really he never was.
(Everyone should know that).

God Is Dead (cont.)

No god, I say, inspired the Book.
Now anyone can write, a kook.
If t'were a god there'd be no wars;
He'd not let men be killed, bear scars.

Now anyone with half a brain
Can see that what I say is sane.
There is no god who cares for me,
My kinfolks and my family.

I wish that they were smart as I.
But though I talk and though I try
They waste their time in futile search
Down in that crowded, little church.

It took no god to make the snow;
To make the little children grow.
Tis natural as the blackest night
Retreating from the dazzling light.

It took no god to make the sun
And give it charted roads to run;
No god to hang the worlds in space;
No god to make my hands, my face.

No God. No God.
There is no God.
Well at least he's dead.
I think.

God Is Kind

Time has a way of doing away with things

but God is kind

for he has at least let us be young

La Push, Washington

111

God loves a
cheerful giver.
God loves all that
we can give
not all that
He gets.

Have You Ever Held a Rose

Have you ever held a rose?

What did you see?

All of you and me

Was in your hand.

(For just at the time

We think that we

Know all of life's dark mysteries

We pale and wither 'fore we can.

Be not too wise.

The rose, the rainfall,

And the sunrise

Are too beautiful to understand.)

Healthy Obsession

I know you saw me see you
but I understand; you did the ladylike thing.
I saw you long before your eyes met mine
Perhaps that's why you're afraid to look again
My eyes could not conceal my heart
and you knew. And you knew I knew you.
Sometimes when you smile
I pretend you're smiling at me
just for fun or maybe, maybe even -- for love.
It makes me happy just to know you're happy
Just to know I can at least see you.
So please allow me my dreams
For without the dream I would have nothing.

Hello, Hallmark

You are very important to me

at this time in my life

for you are a part of my life

an integral part

and should you be lost

a greater part of me would also be lost

so much that I could never again

be what I was

nor ever hope to be

what I could have been

for what I want to be

involves you as much as it does me

for you are more than a friend

you are a part of me

and I am a part of you

and we are each other.

Her First Hour After

She spoke of what might be (or might have been)
And I smiled a wry smile.
She enumerated conditions and consequences,
cause and effect, ad infinitum.
I acknowledged with doubtful grunts.
She expounded on careers, goals, purpose,
reason, fate,
And I heard at least half of it.
It could never work:
Platonic racemizations, stylistic overtures,
Symbolic dialogues, deduced emotions,
Contrived - methodical - rationalized expressions
of a meticulously architectured and compulsively
manufactured relationship.

"Of course" ... "you realize" ... "and furthermore"
Guilt/repression, guilt/repression in a monotonous,
monosyllabic motif.
Imputed, inferred hostility in an ever-widening
crescendo of circumlocutionary rhetoric.
Pleasure-denial in each rigidly structured inflection.
I was all buttoned, tucked, tied and zipped
when she finished; or maybe she finished
because I was.
"This is our beginning," she urged as she
huddled in the blanket.
"Life," I yawned,
"Is but a glimpse of the caboose."

Hereafter

There I lay and God did lay me.
Heaven knows how long I lay.
Years did pass and time decayed me.
Not a breeze did blow my way.

When my vague form passed beneath me,
I took flight, my soul on wings.
Sped through endless halls of mercy.
Saw a hundred unseen things.

High above the clouds below me,
Winged my flight to worlds unknown.
Passed through countless crystal valleys.
Untold wonders I was shown.

As an angel I did journey
Through the endless halls of space.
Like an eagle high and mighty,
Flew I swiftly with all grace.

Gates of Heaven opened for me.
Golden streets I then did trod
To the Holy Throne of Mercy.
Found I there new life with God.

Upper Cataract Lake, Colorado

Hero Unknown

A death-defying gleam
    Paused in a soldier's eye:
A glassy, haunting beam
    Which said, "I will not die"
A wistful, flaunting dream
    That soon would pass on by.

And he stood like a tree
    Which says, "I won't be felled"
An angel on the lea
    Who has no fear of hell
A scout riding carefree
    Upon a dangerous trail.

Then strode there by a breeze
    Which comes before a fight,
Near breathless but with ease
    It cooled the restless night;
A creeping quiet freeze
    Before the morning light.

And when the dawning came
    The soldier was found dead,
A man without a name
    Had for his country bled.
And with no wants of fame,
    "I will," at last he'd said.

Though quiet his body lies,
    His spirit still lives on
And lingers in the skies
    Where laurel twigs are flown.
Somewhere the victor cries
    But he sleeps on unknown.

Hold Your Head up High
The Fundamentalist Perspective - 1967

Hold your head up high
if you must live to die.
If you look down
you're sure to frown
so hold your head up high.

The hawk screams above
but he can't find the dove.
She's nowhere 'round
'cause she looked down
so hold your head up high.

They tell us love each man
as if they think we can.
And when I'm beat
upon the street
they turn their head and sigh.

A "Christian country!"
and yet they say to me
"You can't come in.
We hate your skin."
I turn my head and cry.

The prayer is gone today:
One atheist had her way.
And a million fools
like me and you
can't put it back again.

We say kill Communists
and them we must resist,
in Vietnam,
Laos, or Guam,
but here they're free to stay.

They say that God is dead
and sound just like the Reds
and yet they're praised,
their pay is raised,
and people think they're smart.

O sex is now the queen
in books and magazines
and one big name
who shows no shame
corrupts a million souls.

Hold Your Head up High *(cont.)*

They say that we must fight
because they're wrong, we're right.
They say it too
so I tell you:
the war will never end.

The killers are set free;
the laws say it must be.
You can't confess
or tell them "Yes"
til lawyers tell you "No."

They now have miniskirts
that make us chronic flirts.
They wonder why
divorce is high,
It's because our morals are low.

Got Great Society,
The War on Poverty,
but more than food
and twice as good
we need to share some love.

Hold Your Head up High (cont.)

Then there's them U.F.O.'s
that still nobody knows
where they come from
or where they're gone
or where they're goin' t' be.

They say they are balloons
or maybe yet the moon.
They can't believe
that there might be
someone besides ourselves.

We've fenced our yard up tight
and lock our doors at night
and all in all
we can't recall
our next door neighbor's name.

But we ain't long been here,
let's see, just seven years.
And anyway
we work all day
and nights we have to rest.

Hold Your Head up High *(cont.)*

They never have the time;
can't afford a stamp or dime.
No time for me
or eternity
no time for their funeral.

No time for church we say
we have to rest that day
and yet God gave
us all we have
we're blind with vanity.

Since half the world is "lost"
we bear the Holy Cross
to foreign lands
and heathen bands
forgettin' our own home town.

We see the businessman
flashin' money in his hand.
He'll find his wealth
won't save his self
when God gets ready to judge.

Hold Your Head up High (cont.)

And there's the Ku Klux Klan
a tryin' to save the land
from Black Disgrace
but they hide their face
and they don't act like a man.

There's much that I could say
until my dyin' day
but no one hears
'cause no one cares
so I hold my head up high.

They say that war must be
if we want to be free.
Are we free when we die?
Will you tell me why
I can't hold my head up high?

O yeah, they say be proud;
they shout it long and loud.
Be proud of what?
Be proud we're not
somebody that we've killed?

Hold Your Head up High *(cont.)*

O hold your head up high!
My friend I'm goin' t' try
and hide my tears
forget my fears
and turn my face away.

If I hold my head up high
gotta close my ears and eyes
and make believe
the world's at peace
and doves up in the sky.

Hold your head up high!
Forget the bombed that cry.
Forget the maimed
them left unclaimed,
and hold your head up high.

The sun's up in the sky;
he'll dry that tearful eye.
In all our night
there's somethin' bright:
God's holdin' his head up high.

How Does A Little Flower
by Ken Helton

How does a little flower
Fill up a barren room?
Why does a loved one's welcome
Protect the heart from gloom?

To give a little flower,
Or smile a gentle smile,
Requires the smallest effort
But lasts the greatest while.

Human Nature

some don't forget
some won't forgive
some never yet
as long as they live

some ever steal
some ever lie
some always will
until they die

some go to hell
some go to heaven
some aren't forgot
some aren't forgiven

no man can steal
a place in the sky
no man can make
truth from a lie

Hurrah For the Man With the
Hollow Laugh and the Wooden Face
and the Chiseled Smile

He walks the Basset hound that sleeps in the hall and acknowledges the widow who lives next door -- across the hedge -- with his gruff voice and his rough gentleness.

She stands with her arms crossed at her waist and wonders if he sees her when she prunes the plants.

He wonders if she likes his dog, but, of course, she must. The approach of the hound relieves the conversation as he reaches down and she talks about the marigold seeds. And he looks sidelong with a left eye that's squinted from cigar smoke.

She's flatchested--with a faded grey print dress a little too long, pinned with a gold safety pin a little low cut.

He wonders if she can see without her glasses and she wonders if he wears his.

"I once had a cat . . ."

She looks at the dog and the man grunts, then stands to look toward the street. The Basset hound stands looking down, moving its head with implanted feet; not knowing whether to sit, stand, leave, or hear about the cat.

A car passes by and the man waves as though he knows its passengers, holding his cigar centrally between his teeth to allow a grimace. He leaves his left hand in the air a little long and the widow stares at it.

"I guess I'll have to get the house painted this spring. What color do you think it would look best? (without hesitation) I think blue-grey is a little unfriendly, don't you? But then, white is so commonplace." He grunts with a both-eyed sidelong glance and looks down at the dog again, who looks up with a question. The man dittos it.

Hurrah For the Man (cont.)

The widow rattles on and thinks what a nice man he is but worries whether he keeps the kitchen clean and wonders whether there are ashes in the easy chair and dog hair on the rugs.

She is very slim and erect. He wonders what made her that way, for some reason, assuming that she wasn't always.

She looks at his close-cut, full head of grey hair and wonders if he ever looks at himself in the mirror, and if his bedroom smells of cigars.

While inspecting the inside of his dog's ears, he wonders if her cat is white. The dog moves his front part closer toward him. He rubs the dog more vigorously now.

"Well, Mr. Wherley, I guess I had better be getting back to the house. I have a cake in the oven. It's going to be a German chocolate."

To the dog's surprise, Mr. Wherley stands up quickly and extinguishes his cigar. He runs the palm of his hand from his forehead over his head and then runs one hand around in back beneath his belt to retuck his shirt.

As the widow walks across the lawn, she fastens about her an apron that she has been holding neatly folded in her right hand.

He stares after her with both eyes and a puzzled smile, doesn't feel the dog at his legs, and thinks of, among other things, coffee and German chocolate cake.

I Am Naked

I am naked.
I have no funny face
       to offer the world —
I have no Sunday suit
       to hide my broken heart —
I am what I am —
and I know and God knows —
But for humanity
       I will put on my clothes.

Mount Washington Hotel, New Hampshire

130

I Am With Thee - Art Thou With Me

We came unto an olden land
That stooped in utter poverty
And then my friend asked me again:
"I am with thee - art thou with me?..."

He said that we would see our God
Though now our doubting eyes were blind
And that our bodies would be filled
With water of a different kind.

He led me to the synagogue
Where found we there the Pharisees
Who heard my Lord ask me these words:
"I am with thee - art thou with me?..."

He said though men would scoff and curse
And persecute us night and day,
That God would bless for righteousness
And lead us safely in The Way.

And then he showed me barren fields
And rocky paths beside the sea...
A mighty task, again he asked:
"I am with thee – art thou with me?..."

He pointed to a little bird
And then with saddened eyes he said,
"See here, the sparrow has a nest;
I have no place to lay my head."

At last he led me up a hill,
A hill they still call Calvary.
The scars were white; his voice was quiet:
"I died for thee - art thou with me?..."

So little had he asked me do
And yet so much he offered me,
This man, the Holy Son of God
Who died that now I might be free.

And knowing that I faced my King
I said, "Yes, Lord, I am with thee."
For just a while he gently smiled
And then he said, "Come follow me."

I Etched My Fears

I etched my fears on a slate,
then shattered it into a thousand
pieces to find which one
I had to live first.

I Give A Damn

I give a damn about a few things
I give a damn about Jesus
      and the Father who sent him into the world.
I give a damn about unnecessary and unfruitful wars
I give a damn about people starving to death
I even give a damn about people stuffing to death
Why the hell not?
If I don't care about you
Why should you care about me
      and vice versa?
Love thy neighbor as thy self
      or at least
Do unto others as you would have them do unto you.
So why not?
What's wrong with everyone getting the same breaks?
(and everyone helping to mend them?)

I Had a Friend

I had a friend who had a friend
who had a friend.
And once that I had told the lie
It did not end.

No longer now the friend
I had so long is mine,
Because for just a few short words,
I was unkind.

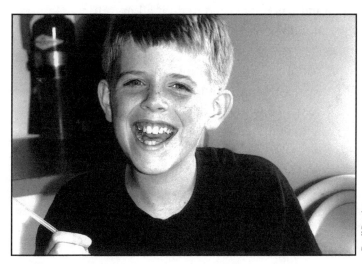

Geoff Bowles

I Know This God of Mine is Real

I know this god of mine is real
for he's a thing that I can feel.
He lives down deep within my hungry soul.
He makes my frazzled life be whole.

All of my life, all of my life,
searching but I couldn't find
someone who cared about me
with nothing else in mind.

I know that he is in control;
I'm thankful 'cause sometimes I'm not;
and when I've tried to do it all myself,
It didn't turn out very hot.

All of my life, all of my life,
searching but I couldn't find
someone who cared about me
with nothing else in mind.

Suddenly there is new hope;
suddenly there is brave joy.
Fears of desertion have melted away;
not lonely though sometimes alone.

I Live in the Land of Stone

I live in the land
    Of stone
And though there are millions at hand
    I live alone

I have been here long
    Unknown
And all the thousand youthful songs
    I knew are gone

I don't laugh like
    Before
And all emotions, pride, and faith
    abide no more

I move in perpetual
    Motion
And all my aims and hopes are lost
    In the commotion

Each day, the same as
    the past
Rushes before me blindingly fast

Oh lost am I to
    myself
for I've no self respect no pleasures left

yes, I just exist

I Live in the Land of Stone *(cont.)*

No thought
for others and bathed in wealth I'm
hell bought

condemn me not you
Who know
you who live in nature's love
and grow

for I've been dwarfed
in all
by monsters of stone too big and
too tall

My world's dark and grey
and numb
it hears nor sees nor feels and
Is dumb

it speaks but yet with
no words
and what is uttered dies and is
not heard

by me, I who live
alone
Here in this land, this friendless land
of stone.

I saw a child crying today
not out of hunger
not for love
not for clothes
not out of sickness
       but because his brother's boat
       was prettier than his
and I thought a long while
and I didn't smile and I didn't frown
my heart was in Biafra
my mind in Vietnam
my eyes in New York City

     my voice in the sea

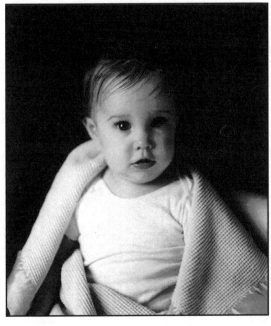

1320 Southedge, Little Rock, Arkansas

139

I Shall Return

I shall return when spring comes round.
And apple blossoms wing the breeze;
When grass roots shoot up through the
ground
and birds and leaves are clothing trees.
It is a happy time I hear
when lovers walk and hearts do burn
And when there's mirth and fewer tears
I shall return.

My body lies upon the snow
Beneath a cold and threat'ning sky
In fairer fields, where warm winds blow
I wished to die, my form to lie.
My anxious soul impatient grows
For warming rays of sun I yearn
And when they come and cool lakes glow
I shall return.

I Want To Close My Eyes

I want to close my eyes
in the sleep of the future
and carry with me a journey of the past
that I might awake
in the presence of the morrow,
a wiser man,
an humbler soul.

I'll Be With You
Matt. 11:28-30

Come to me all you who labor
All you who are heavy laden
Come to me all you who toil
With the weight of the world.

Take my yoke upon you
I will make it light
I'll be with you around the curve
With you through the night.

With you in the toughest times
With you in the worst of times
I'll be with you
and you'll know I'm there
'cause you know I care.

I'll be with you always
Even when you think I'm not
There's no rest for me
Until you're home again.

Because I released you
Many years ago from here
And things have not been the same
Since you've been away.

I think about you night and day
I'm praying for you now
I love the way you talk to me
I love the way you bow.

I'll Be With You *(cont.)*

I love the way you call my name
I loved it when you released your shame
I'll be with you
and you'll know I'm there
'cause you know I care.

I'll be with you round the curve
With you through the night
In the darkest thunderstorm
I'll provide a light.

I'll be with you
and you'll know I'm there
'cause you know I care.

If Ever I Live To Be Old

When my road of life is ending,
And my form is stooping, bending,
And my words are all offending,
     let me bid the world good'bye.

When my body's weak and aching,
And my hands are trembling, shaking,
And my heart in sorrow's breaking,
     God see fit to let me die.

When there's tottering to my walking,
And there's stammering in my talking,
And the children me are mocking,
     may my dawn of death be nigh.

When they're tired of comfort giving,
And I'm wholly tired of living,
And they're tired of me forgiving,
     may they then not have to try.

When I'm tired of drinking, eating,
And my heart is slowly beating,
And the days are rushing, fleeting,
     let me close my failing eyes.

When I'm ever hurting, ailing,
And my eyesight's swiftly failing,
And my wrinkled face is paling,
     God send solace from the sky.

If I Could Sing

Lord, if I could sing
with a great voice
if I could get your ear
way down here on the earth
I'm just a little speck
but I know you know me
The hairs upon my head you know.

If I could be a man
Not just any kind of man
If I could tell your story far and wide
and be in demand.
Well you know I would
if I only could
and it would be so good,
so very good.

If I had a voice
that I could sing
that I could express just anything
everything you've done for me
and everything you do
if I could tell it right
if I could tell it true
Oh, you know I would
if I only could
and it would be so good
so very good,
so very good.

If I Could Sing (cont.)

And if I could dream
Oh, you know I'd dream
I would tell it all:
How it was and how it seemed
and I know you're there
and I know you care.
If I only could your presence
right now share.

I'm lifting holy hands
The tears are running down
and if I strain to hear
I think they're angel sounds
I really don't know,
I don't know what they're like
but could I hear them anyway?

I'm lifting holy hands
The tears are running down
and if I strain to hear
I think they're angel sounds
for I know you care
and I know you speak
and I can hear you now
that still voice strong, not weak,
saying,

"Let me love you
Let me love you
Don't need to talk more
just simply listen
and let my arms enfold you
and let my wings enfold you
and let my love simply mold you."

146

If I Could Sing (cont.)

If I had a voice
I would gladly sing
I would tell the whole world anything
Everything about you
Everything so grand
and they would want to clap
and they would want to stand.

We're raising holy hands
The tears are flooding down
and if I strain to hear
it sounds like angel sounds.
I really don't know what they sound like
but I'm sure you do
And you'll let me hear
And you'll let me hear
just what I need
just what I need
just what I need
to know.

If Time Stood Still

If time stood still for just a day,
The idle peace would let minds stray
From duty, rush, and petty goals,
That warp men's minds and starve their souls.

Ah, restless life, thy bird on wing,
Why dost thou not a new song sing,
Of tranquil days and restful night?
And then somewhere thou couldst alight.

But here within this loathesome world
The many darts of hate are hurled,
Are hurled at you, O hapless life,
Born but to fears and endless strife.

Oh, woe, thy wayfarer from God
When he to Gabriel shall nod
And loud and clear that clarion call
Shall slow us all, yea, slow us all.

If You See Me

If you see me someday thither
somewhere somewhy on your road
Lest apart we both should wither
Let us share our common load.

And though self prevail against us
Let us yield to the demands
Understanding, hope, and trust
happy hearts and helping hands.

And alas when time is giving
Death the key to our life's door
Will be said such friends in living
And in dying all the more.

Arkansas River, Wichita, Kansas

149

Implications of Commitment

Lips have not known greater passion
nor fingers yet such fire.
Hands have never held such throbbing
as their bold desire.

Minds are free with mad abandon
to feel the surge, the pain;
to count the value of the moment,
not future loss or gain.

Quick hands reach out and grasp
a body warm and clutching too:
sweaty, oozing, spurting, smelling;
groping tight they do.

Plastered by their drying juices,
they both wipe their hands;
wrinkled, naked, spent and breathless,
each one slowly stands.

Evasive eyes reveal the spoilage
where their passions lay,
and thinking each an

                empty

                      thought,

they turn and run away.

In Search of Many

In search of many
I found few
To help me with my work.
In fact I only
Found me two;
The others seemed to smirk.

When I got money
And my rank,
The two I forgot.
Now all the many
Were my friends
And yet the two were not.

In the Quiet Hours

Somedays I still awake
searching for you.
My hand seeks out your being
eagerly
but in vain.
And soon I turn again with a sigh
to the sleep that never returns.

I lie in bed on my back
and watch the ceiling grow lighter
with dawn
and it almost gives me hope:
Perhaps, this day will bring you—
but, I know, it cannot be.

I remember how I held you
        in the mornings;
your small breasts gently caressed
        my heart
telling it all I wanted to hear—
with a clenched fist I strike the empty mattress
and bury my face in a pillow:
"God! Man should not have to sleep alone!"

In the Quiet Hours

Yesterday when I came home from work
I almost expected you would be there with a kiss
and when you were not I called your name.
I even thought I heard you in the kitchen
and smelled coffee.
But maybe, perhaps, I just dreamed it.

It is in the quiet hours
that I am most aware of your absence,
the hours we had together,
the hours that were once yours and mine,
that now are only mine----
    and God's.

Inevitable
by Ken Helton and Mark Bowles

The lightning flashed and in the sky,
Along each cloud the thunder crept.
Through piney woods and meadow green,
The wind, like an avenger swept;
And on each face an ashen sheen,
Yet no one fled but rooted stood
As if some voice from Hades called
And bade them be the devil's cud.

Then from the storm's tempestuous depths,
There came a sad, uncertain roar
As though the wind reluctant felt
To take a mortal life once more.
But nature's forces each are dealt
A course which they must follow through
And lowly man, in ruined land,
Has always made his life anew.

Yet some have laughed and mocked the tide
Which rolls at last to cover all,
And they have met their certain end
Amidst that clear and tireless call.
Ah! fate sounds loud upon the wind
Her plan of joy, of peace, and strife;
And all will follow at her sound
In caravans – to death or life.

Internship
1975

I'm snared by an occupation with preoccupations
That squander all the time I can borrow or steal.
I'm giving myself to everyone else but you!
You love me in absentia
While I'm curing Ms. Jones' dementia,
And you're always waiting for me at the door.
I come home to find my little girl knows twenty new
words,
three new birds, the meaning of love, and my first
name.

I'm programmed to be a physician,
To assess the patient's condition; Heart and liver,
Psyche and soul, diagnosis, prognosis,
Climb every mountain,
Explore every hole.
Getting down to earth, being father and husband
Can be like getting out of character.

The Valentine tulips have long since wilted in the vase
Without the flowers of Springtime to put in their place.
I've been incarcerated with the infirm,
Protected but neglected, I'm cut off from the world
And sometimes from you.

It's Funny How Friendships Fade

It's funny how friendships fade
Like the sun into the shade
Something we thought we'd never trade
It's funny how friendships fade.

It's funny how friendships fade
Just like they were never made
As though their value's never weighed
It's funny how friendships fade.

It's funny how friendships fade
As though foundations were never laid
As though to share, we are afraid
It's funny, so funny, how friendships
fade.

Whidbey Island, Washington

J. P. Johnson

"I'm going to die!" J. P. Johnson told the nurse. "And that Paul Wilson will become President of my company. Oh no! Not that! Wilson, President of Yum Yum Dog Food....ha, ha, ha, ha...ha, ha...."

Here the old gentleman broke into a mania of hysterical laughter. The nurse tried to calm him but he began again:

"Why Paul Wilson, that moron... he doesn't even know how the dog biscuits taste. I believe in knowing your product. If you manufacture dog food, eat it; if you make handkerchiefs use them; or girdles wear .... Oh, I'm going to die! I know it!"

"Mr. Johnson," the nurse began, "did you say you ate Yum Yum dog food?"

"Yes, of course!" he barked. "It's just like..."

"Yes, I know... like using a handkerchief or wearing a girdle. No wonder you had a fifteen-foot long tapeworm."

"Is that a record?" Mr. Johnson seemed to come out of his swoon for a moment. Then he cried out, "I'm going to die! Mother! Mother!"

"Here, here," the young nurse said, "control yourself. You're not going to die."

"Yes, I am " the tycoon boomed and then assuming a feeble voice he repeated, "yes, I am. You know it. You're just trying to make me feel good."

Then Mr. Johnson looked around the room at the many flowers which had been sent to him by employees. He raised up on one arm: "And those flowers. They just bought them now so they wouldn't have to later — for my funeral. Get them out of here! Get them out!"

157

J. P. Johnson *(cont.)*

Here he fell backwards, exhausted. The nurse prepared to give him a sedative and told him to quiet himself. But like a chicken who must have another round after his head is cut off, he started talking again:

"Just think, I should be eating a steak now. Instead I'm eating pain pills."

"This is a sedative, Mr. Johnson."

"Yes, that's it. Let me sleep right into eternity." Mumbling, he finally fell asleep.

That evening he awoke. He did not see the nurse refilling the water pitcher.

"Just as I thought," he said in a voice like that of a magician, "I thought purgatory would be like this."

Then the nurse said, "Mr. Johnson..."

"Who are you!" the bedladen, tapeworm-ridden, tycoon exploded.

"I'm one of the nurses on this floor."

"What heaven?" Mr. Johnson asked.

"I beg your pardon sir?"

"I asked you, what heaven. You know... fourth, fifth... like that."

"Mr. Johnson, you are on the second floor of Blair General Hospital."

To that answer he frowned.

The nurse looked queerly at Mr. Johnson for awhile and then said:

"Mr. Johnson, are you ill?"

"Well, I guess so," he replied "or else I wouldn't be in the hospital." The nurse turned up her nose and stalked out of the room.

In his convalescent period, when he was getting

better, J. P. Johnson got graver and gloomier every day. In his private ward he had access to a telephone, and on one of his moodiest days he made a call to his Vice-President Paul Wilson. He told Paul to take the office of president of the Yum Yum company that day, and that because of ill health and a trip, he would no longer be able to perform his duties. Then with a feeling of sympathy for all the scattered, homeless, hungry children of the world, he called up his bank. He told the President to remove his money from his savings account and deposit it in the various charity funds of New York. There went J. P. Johnson's fortune and many mouths were filled, hurts were helped, and hearts made jubilant. Mr. Johnson was expecting his departing hour any moment one day when Dr. Thrasher entered his room.

"Mr. Johnson, I have some good news for you."

"Yes, I know." the great donor calmly said.

"You do?" the doctor asked with an odd look on his face. "You can get ready any time."

"My dear doctor," Johnson replied in a fatherly voice, "I've been ready for two weeks."

"Then you can get dressed."

"I am dressed. I want to go like this."

"Like that? But you would be breaking the law!"

"The law?" Mr. Johnson asked incredulously. "What do you mean by that remark?"

"Well if we release you from this hospital, you must be dressed in something besides pajamas."

"Leave the hospital... release..." Mr. Johnson mumbled.

J. P. Johnson *(cont.)*

"Yes," said the doctor jubilantly. "You're in perfect health!"

"But I can't be, I'm dying! Can't you see I'm dying!" Here Mr. Johnson broke into an hysterical fit of laughter. Any longer and he would have been committed to the neurotic ward. But he finally got dressed. Walking down the halls he mumbled: "I'm penniless... I'm no longer president... I won't be able to buy dog biscuits... or dog food." And then he would break into an hysterical fit of laughter. Out of the hospital and down Broadway he walked.

After about three blocks he came to the South Baptist Relief Mission. There was a huge crowd of ragged-clad men who looked as if they would drop dead of malnutrition any moment. They were reading or trying to read a huge sign at the front of two long "breadlines." As he wandered closer to the encircled sign where women were dishing out soup and bread, he saw his name in big letters:

FOOD FURNISHED THREE TIMES
A DAY FOR NINE MONTHS
TO COME BY J. P. JOHNSON

J. P. Johnson *(cont.)*

He gave ear to the conversation and heard his name
called over and over.

"That J. P. Johnson must be a real great guy."

"Yeh."

"J. P. Johnson... what a man!"

"Maybe we can pay him back some day."

Then our hero pushed out his chest like a songbird
and said:

"I'm J. P. Johnson."

A few laughed at him and astounded at their
disbelief, he repeated:

"I am J. P. Johnson! I am!"

A white-headed old man said: "Sure. I'm Napoleon."
Then others chimed in saying, "I'm Paul Revere. I'm
George Washington." Then our hapless chariter began
screaming; then crying; then saying "Mother, Mother."

Even when the men in white suits came with strait
jacket and paddy wagon he was still mumbling:

"I am J. P. Johnson... I am Johnson... I am."

Je Regrette Tout

What is a day after it's gone:

nothing but wisdom we should have known

nothing but deeds we should have done

nothing but victories we should have won

nothing but friends we should have made

nothing but truths we should have weighed

nothing but facts we learned too late

A day is a deed that was too long ago

Jesus Christ the Human-God

I remember days gone by
When Lazarus died, I saw you cry
When children came I saw you laugh
I saw love in your eyes.

People hurt and I saw you care
When things went wrong you were always
there
You taught us how to look to God
Taught us how to share.

And you taught us how to pray
Taught us how to walk your way
And how to love our fellow man
You taught us what to say.

And someday you'll come again
Sure as day or night or rain
And what we lose in this life now
Will be tomorrow's gain.

From now through eternity
Your loving arms encircle me
And you guide me every step;
My soul you've gladly kept.

Just a Police Action
by Ken Helton

It was just a peaceful little War
With no-one being killed.
A few were shot to death and some say
They died and never lived again.
But these were exceptions to the general
Rule of "Live and let die."
They said it was a "police action;"
Gave them wooden guns, clay swords,
And told them to attack.
A lot said "no" and were shot;
A lot did and they died too.
But this was still just a "police action"
And those who died were
"courageous volunteers;"
But they were still dead.

McConnel AFB, Wichita, Kansas

Just Call me Sir

I have no name just call me "Sir"
And let me go about my way.
Don't ask my name just call me "Sir"
And let me be but that today.
I go no place just call it "there"
And let me now be on my way.
Don't ask the place just call it "there"
And let it be but that today.
I have no age just call them "years"
And let me live a year today.
My life's been plagued by grief and tears;
That's why my hair has now turned gray.
Don't ask me "How?" just call it "life"
And that is all that we will say.
Don't question "What?" just call it "strife"
And let me go my way today.
You wonder! Just forget you saw
And heard this grieving gray-haired man.
Just call me "Sir", it "there" and "years".
That's life. Forget me if you can.

Just for Fun

The sound of a heart that was weeping
I heard through the old inn door
A maiden fair was weeping
weeping and weeping some more

I said my dear, "What is the cause
of such a heavy heart?
I have not seen in all my life
such that tears one apart."

And with just a hint of soft laughter
The barmate threw her a dime
She said, with eyes a twinkling,
"You see it works everytime."

Keep All Your Tears

Keep all your tears for another day
Don't shed them here,
Smile all those frowns away
Have no fear.
The world is weighted down with woe
And breaking underneath its bow
So keep all your tears.

Keep all your sighs for another night
Don't voice them yet,
Somewhere morns still are bright –
Please don't forget.
The world is spitting prayers of hate
So love your neighbor 'fore it's too late.
We're dying slowly if we wait,
The hand of time shall write our fate
So keep all your sighs.

Keep all your tears, keep all your sighs
Forget the one called self,
Don't yield to laud and lies
You're not the last one left.
The whole big world is near
So lonely through the years,
Just waiting for your smile,
A kindly word awhile.
Keep all your tears, keep all your tears.

Kevin
9-13-78

Kevin is four,
with big brown eyes
and needle tracks
and a fuzzy head
and a birthday next
month.

He doesn't like doctors
or the hospital
or Memphis
and who could blame him.
He seems to understand a lot.

Good luck, Kevin.

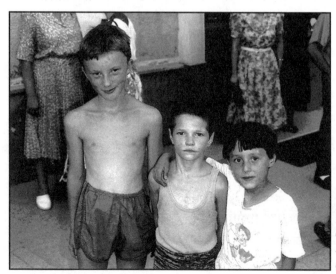

Oradea, Romania

Lament for Felicity

Felicity, where have you gone?
O please return unto our home,
And heal this breaking heart of mine
With your soft touch, O one divine.
This house was filled with happiness,
With laughter, and with thankfulness,
Until my loved one you did fade
Into the mings and ev'ning shade.

I've searched for you about the land,
In every town throughout Japan,
And weeping now I pray for you
And humbly now I wait for you.

Our son has gone away to war,
To fight and die somewhere afar,
And now you've left me here alone
Within this house that once had shone
As bright as rising sun with love
Now dark as starless skies above.

Last Days of Youth

I sat upon an oaken bough
Beside a silver lane,
Which ran along the landlord's fields,
All full of golden grain.

It was the early morning time
When all the world was fresh;
The same old sun appeared again
To gently warm my flesh.

The summer now had run away,
Like children having fun,
And left the rest of us behind –
Who had nowhere to run.

The birds that sang, the winds that blew;
The sea that ran to shore,
Said, You must have somewhere to go,
Now linger here no more.

I climbed down from my tree of dreams
And left sweet youth behind,
For dreams are useless if they stay
Within a person's mind.

Laughter-Man
(to Tom Cain, MD, London Sabbatical, 1979)

You are mirth-from-birth
Mr. Laugh-Man.

My own private clown.
You keep my eyes wet with joy,
erase my frowns.
You integrate wit and wisdom
conviviality and vision.

A jester
as in days of old.
You erase the pain, stop the clock,
shut out the cold.

Lighthearted, devoted,
the timid soul cries out
with zany abandon when you speak;

Sometimes the treatment lasts for weeks.
But now I peer down empty halls
at silent faces on the walls;
unspoken feelings vex us all.

Beneath the breast, hearts burn
for the Laughter-man,
For your return.

LBJ

This is the Administration
Beagle dogs and integration
Hairless heads and roaming noses
Tailess hounds and swollen toeses
Aid in time of true disaster
Planes that fly real far and faster
War on poverty and dumbness
Energy for social numbness
Great societies and cities
Constant Aid, and tears, and pity
Welfare checks and compensation
Summit talks and calm negations
Saving dough by turning lights out
Boosting all by going nights out
Putting down the worlds' rebellions
Making them as bad as hellion.

Letter from Brother

Dear Mark,

I drew your name
oh! woe is me
What shall I put
beneath your tree?
And then to my joy I see
a list that you prepared for me.
Gloves, umbrella and Pierre Cardin.
So shopping I went again & again
Umbrellas, yes but what a cost
Pierre Cardin - he must be lost
So enjoy these gloves and poetry bit
Oh! My gosh, I hope they fit.

Love you all
Happiest of Christmases

Geoff

Lewis Carroll
Logic and Nails

Yes, fingernails are miracles
And how they interest me
For if we did not have them
They would be hard to see

But if we had not had them
or, say we had forgot,
It would be odd to see them
now tell me would it not?

But if no one had seen them
or even ever heard
NAILS would not be a poem
or even yet a word.

Life is a Rat Race
(First page lost)

Who lost a rat
Under a hat
Without a band
Atop the sand.
I had the band
Inside my hand.
I took the hat;
Replaced the band.
Then ran the rat
Chased by the cat.
I found a pan
All full of sand
Beside a can
Atop the land,
Where ran the cat,
the Man, the rat,
Where lay the band
Atop the sand.
I found a fan;
The cat again
Who caught the rat
Next to a bat.
Gave him a pat,
Picked up the bat,
The band, the hat,
the pan, the cat,
the fan, some sand,

Life is a Rat Race *(cont.)*

And there I sat.
Then came the Man;
Found me again
Atop the sand.
He took his hat
And band, the cat
(Who ate the rat),
The bat, the pan,
And waved his hand.
Then there I sat
Atop the sand.
I got a tan,
A worn-out fan,
And rusty can.

Ocean City, Maryland

176

Lines

Lines, lines, endless lines
On my father's face
And I know that some are mine
I put them in their place

Tears, tears, silver tears
In my mother's eye
And I see that through the years
I often made her cry

Scars, scars, thorny scars
On my master's brow
He got them on the hill of Mars
And bears them for me now.

Male Climacteric

Call it male climacteric or whatever you like; but eventually duty overrides passion. A singular pursuit preempts other responsibilities and relationships to the point that the intensity is exhausting.

Achievement in this area gives one headstrong giddiness but occasionally one is left atop a flagpole thrashed about in the wind.

Work is an adequate opiate, mistress, parent, friend, god and avocation – until it seems reasonable, bearable; then filling the extra time becomes threatening, unsettling.

Superficial investments in relationships do not suddenly achieve flourishing fruition. Relaxation has no definition; is not in the vocabulary or lifestyle.

Suddenly one feels unsuccessful, threatened, even frightened. Loss of self esteem creeps in as work intensity or success has been the major measure of self actualization/realization. It has been the chief priority.

The lack of continuous industry can lead to self deprecation, dissatisfaction.

The deprioritized family must go on with their lives, incomplete. Are we not important? Can't you give us some of this energy?

Only a strong sense of duty can justify a withdrawal from the intensity. Is it a reason or a rationalization? What will I think of myself if I withdraw? Can I withdraw even in the face of overwhelming needs? *Yes.* I must.

God give me your best while I try to give you and my family mine.

Marriage Encounter
1981

You were young and said "yes" before you knew
what demands life held for you.

Susan, I loved you.

Susan, I have enjoyed this time with you. I don't
have anything poetic or eloquent to write except --
I love you -- always will -- and look forward to living
with you -- somewhere -- forever.

I believe we complement each other perfectly and that
God ordained our meeting and marriage. Although we
have much to learn from God, I believe he will make
it as atraumatic as possible. I believe God has plans
for our lives - to be instruments of his grace, love,
peace and mercy. I believe we can give credibility to
his purpose.

He has richly blessed us, filled us with his spirit,
poured out his love and blessings, answered our
prayers and fulfilled our dreams.

I love you for being the person, woman, wife and
mother you are. I would not change you radically in
any way - if at all.

I love your anguish, your anger, your joy, your tears,
your peace and frustration. I love your vigor of
thought, your revolutionary notions.

Marriage Encounter *(cont.)*

This time of silence and reflection has been good for me, for us, for our children, for our acquaintances, for the patients.

I feel refreshed and stronger; renewed and relieved by the similarity of our responses; by your cognizance of those responses without us declaring them.

I love our simple day-to-day existence and our future expectations. Thank God for good friends. Help us to be a friend to those around us. I want to (foremost and primarily) be your good friend. I hope you will call me when you need me; need me when you have problems; have problems if you don't need me.

I ask you to accept the things you like about me and be honest about the qualities you dislike. I ask for your suggestions and patience regarding the latter.

I want to always be your husband, friend, the father of your children, your lover, advocate, your coworker, playmate and sounding board.

Don't shun me with silence when you need to talk. Don't talk to me when you need silence. Don't assume I will understand you since I've known you a long time. Assume, however, that I will *always truly love you.*

Mayflie

Mayflie, mayflie
Live but to die;
Flit fast your fragile wings.
Night's rest is nigh.

If God made the sparrow gay
And gave him more than one warm day,
I wonder why it is your fate
To live but just a day.

May Love Be Yours

While walking through the woods one day,
I came upon true love.
The sun was laughing in its warmth;
The skies were blue above.

And there they were as lovers are:
Entranced in gentle sighs.
And many stories yet unheard
They told me with their eyes.

So close they were I said, "How sweet
If all mankind were thus:
United, sharing all their needs.
What hope there'd be for us!"

They then looked up and smiled at me
(What ills compassion cures!)
And took they both my hands in theirs
And said, "May love be yours."

Me

Somewhere there's a spirit running free;
Someone like me
Without restraints, regards, regret
Running yet.

Getting old but not older
More cautious but bolder
Alive and awake with each breath that I take —
Running free; autonomy.

Abhorred by the system I,
appalled by its wisdom,
Low-profile and quiet
But still all will see
A man who is right;
running free.

Miscarriage

The laughter of two apparent drunks on the street corner seemed profane. I worried about you. You sat with your chin on baby's head staring ahead, but I don't think you could see out the windshield.

It was a blank, ominous stare.

I hated to leave you, but I had to make the call. It was 2:30 a.m.

Dr. Viala was already at the hospital - seeing another patient - which seemed both good and bad. Good that he was available; bad that I couldn't get immediate, undivided attention for you.

I was afraid you would fall apart physically as we walked in. Baby was still asleep - on my left shoulder as I supported you with my right arm. I had forgotten you were barefoot. You didn't say a word.

I imagined for a brief moment we were entering church or a relative's home; and I envisioned how happy everyone would be to see us.

We had to sit down and give much information to a thin lady who was superficially nice but had a poor memory. After this inquiry, we were informed that Dr. Viala had gone home some minutes before.

I was crushed.

The nurse said she would call him "in 10 to 15 minutes after he's had time to get home."

Tears appeared on your face again, and I too felt like I could cry.

Baby woke up with a big smile. She was soothed back to sleep with a bottle of milk.

The small Christmas tree in the waiting room seemed almost sacred and warm in contradistinction to the cold, wet night.

They called for you to come back to a small room to get undressed. I overheard the nurse: "She's from Waldo. She says you delivered their last baby... No she's OK. Well OK. Bye-bye."

184

Miscarriage *(cont.)*

It seemed like an eternity. Finally I walked over and asked, "What did he say?"

"Since it's 3:00 a.m., he is going to wait a few hours and see her about 7:30."

"But...but...but."

"Well your wife's not in any great distress. She is just having a miscarriage."

My lips began to tremble as something warm welled up in my eyes. I briskly walked outside with baby sleeping in my arms. I realized I was holding my breath. I exhaled and then took in a deep breath as tears rushed profusely from my cheeks onto the sidewalk.

When I went back inside, a nurse was standing beside you, talking - about her five grandchildren, her four children, and her two miscarriages. "God knows best. Anyway it's better to lose a blighted baby early than late. My mother always said, if it was a good baby you could jump off the roof and not shake it loose."

It was almost inhumane.

You were forcing your gentle, delicate smile in an utmost act of surrender to everything and everybody. You seemed stripped of all dignity and self worth. You seemed completely beaten and submissive. My heart ached.

Seven-thirty came and Dr. Viala was a man of his word. The work was brief, but painful. They said it was a boy.

Baby was hungry and out of milk. A nurse acquired a half- pint. She also found a diaper.

You were so weak - but lovely. At least it was over. We probably could not have borne the strain an hour longer. It was tragic but at least we knew where we stood.

In the waning amber light of dusk we sped along the dusty road, as lightning flashed in the eastern sky and the air smelled of rain. The bad left back tire was bumping. You were humming a soft lullaby.

Miscarriage *(cont.)*

Baby was already asleep on your lap.

My billfold was empty, but I felt stronger than ever and I knew God would provide.

A railroad train pierced the night with its noise and light, delaying the journey. The car stalled as we counted the 78th car.

It began to rain as I looked under the hood, pretending I knew something to make you feel better. The rain dropped off the end of my nose. You forced a smile through the rain-beaded windshield. I delayed for fear of failure. The caboose passed into the gulf of darkness and left no residual light or sound. The lightning abated and only a sound downpour gave voice to the ebony night. The silence was depressing. It seemed a miracle that the ole crate had started. Obscuring the dense impersonalization of the night, you squeezed my hand and I kissed your cheek, which had hidden a lingering tear. I hugged you as baby slept. We rode, seemingly, for an eternity - in silence except for the monotonous swish of windshield wipers. We met no cars.

Finally we arrived in town just as the rain stopped. A few neons were still lit giving an uncanny appearance to the rain-polished streets.

The town was impressively empty, deserted.

The experience was a cathartic one. Having shared it we were closer than ever before. Therefore in our loss there was gain; and our cause for sorrow fostered an ultimate greater happiness.

Not a cloud graced the stark blue sky as we ambled home. The sun was almost warm in its touch. Baby slept soundly in the seat as our hands met for a firm squeeze. A relaxed smile arched your face and your eyes spoke palpable words.

A flock of blackbirds flew up as the left back tire went tapping up the highway.

Mission, KS
1987

The elevated sidewalk that threw me on my face on Johnson Drive one night is still there with summer grass underneath its shelf.

It knocked the breath out of me. People affect people like that sometime.

Cold ice water in two discrete trails rolling down the center of your back....

I know you hate chalk on your hands but a pineapple sundae will make it better. And

I don't think you should worry about what you see. There are some things about the way God made us that we just have to accept. Remember, all the good points; a lot of those are covered up for some reason. But mysteries are OK.

You are on your front steps, about two steps up, bare feet even and toes scrunching the sidewalk. Your cat is beside you. You suddenly look up because the cat looks up and I'm driving by in that old blue car with the top down. I say, "I didn't know you were back home", and you say "Gosh, where have you been?" and I say something irrelevant and imprecise like "God only knows".

You say, "Well, I've missed you."

"Thanks!"

"So what are you doing?"

"Oh nothing."

"How's your family?"

"Oh great, just great."

"Have you been home..er uh..to see your parents lately?"

"Last weekend."

"How are they?"

"Fine."

"Good."

"And how are you?"

"Ok. I'm okay"

"Good."

For a brief flash our souls meet. (The ice water reaches the bottom of your back and suddenly I cannot breathe.)

187

Monastic Manners

The heads were shaved
And feet were laved
For clean and better thinking
And with clothed feet
We now can eat
For feet are not a'stinking

San Diego Zoo, California

Mr. Green

Once I had a next door neighbor;
Never did I know his name.
I was busy with my labor
And my useless bids for fame.

So when today there came a lady
Collecting money at my door
"For Mr. Green who died last night,"
I knew not whom the wreath was for.

Musings on the Passionate Man

A man of passion can do dramatic things – dramatically good or bad. His intensity either provokes intense dislike or affection. His enthusiasm particularly disturbs the sedate, the proper, the conservative. He puts into words from a personal perspective what some would be embarrassed to think. He is vulnerable but, paradoxically, generally successful. He has difficulty with men of strong egos, with men who have an intellectual understanding of calamity but are short on empathy, mercy, sensitivity. He has a capacity for brilliance and excellence given the right milieu, but has the likelihood of withering to an insignificant shrivel if constricted, ignored, passed over.

His adaptability and capacity to change are probably remarkable, but transitions are more chaotic and flamboyant because of the fervor. The heat of the fire sometimes burns people. The passionate man does not seem real. He is branded as a maniac, an actor, an addict, even deranged. However, in time the initial chaos subsides and the positive passion becomes more manifest. In the interim, however, some do not know the passionate man. They have not known such a man. They are defensive, the protectorate of humankind, the purgers of the misfits and impaired. Their cruel sentence may have euphemistic, even friendly, trappings but merciless finality. They will never be comfortable with the passionate man. They will not be able to find reasons to like a man who is unpredictable. Their desire is order, control, design, careful planning. The passionate man can rely on these but also appropriates improvisation, intuition, emotion.

These seem dangerously intangible to the dispassionate man. The dispassionate man evinces understanding in verbiage and form but becomes exasperated with the agonies of interpersonal emotions. The dispassionate man sees this intense soul as an economic liability because of his intense effects on people — some potentially negative.

The passionate man is a poor spectator. He is a player, a performer; when reined in he becomes introspective, depressed. He needs to be productive and to touch people's lives and have them touch him. His motivation is usually not money. It could be zeal to achieve, learn, influence, affect, exhort, teach; but not to exploit, manipulate, badger, discourage. He may be particularly loyal to the underprivileged, the underdog, the truthful. This may rail against the common good, the orderly fashion, the central committee. With so many spotlights focused on the passionate man, he becomes scrutiny for many. Vigilance always yields some negative returns. The passionate man takes chances and occasionally fails. His failure is unforgivable and unconscionable to the dispassionate because he did not play by their rules.

Only a passionate man can understand a passioniate man.

My Brother
1957

My brother lies
Deep so deep
Under his tombstone
Fast asleep.

Memories of him
Make me cry,
I remember the day
That he did die.

Struck by car
I saw him fall;
I ran to the house
"Come mother!" I called.

We ran to the corner
Where he did lay.
"Oh, mother, help me!"
He did say.

All cut and bruised
And bleeding to death,
I watched him, slowly,
Lose his breath.

The funeral bells
Rang the next day
But I knew brother
Had gone to heaven to stay.

My Brother
1992

You are my brother.
I remember how you carried
me on your shoulders
I was probably five or six
 and you were twenty
Through deep dark woods
With screech owls calling
I held on tight no fear
          no light
The early AM moon had not
yet risen
to grace the bullfrogs'
          cacophonous cry
and trace the serpentine
course of cottonmouth
moccasins on night
maneuvers with you and I
          felt your whiskers and
your early bald spot
          I knew you were a
hero, you were my brother
If I close my eyes I can
feel the anticipation I felt as
a kid when I knew you were
coming home
          I can still see you standing
in the sunlight and feel
you tickling
my tummy with your red beard

193

My Brother *(cont.)*

   I remember how the seaweed
cookies tasted (salty!)
and how the
music box smelled and how the
yen looked and felt and smelled
   I remember the glass blowgun
was my pride & joy as were the
balanced throwing knife, gyroscope
and Canon camera
   I remember your letters calling
me "bud" and mine to you
signed "little brother"
   your army shirt I
wore way up into college
When I was 16 and you were 30
we spotlighted
to see what we could find
in the delta night
We shot 22 rifles at hawks in
giant cypress trees a half mile
away with little hope of ever
finding the right trajectory
   We hunted frogs with
carbide headlamps giving off
pungent odors making us
look like miners caught
in some eerie
shaft unseen forgotten

My Brother *(cont.)*

We hunted snakes and you
wrestled them in the
murky water while I stood frozen
still
You careened cars
down the sides of
levees defying gravity and sanity
you had no fear so I had
little - after all you were my brother
We sit here now in your
warm shop
with the cold Oklahoma wind
outside

14 Bluebird Lane, Bentonville, Arkansas

My Brother (cont.)

I am definitely middle-aged
and you are pushing 58
Your strong neck is
supported by a brace
recent surgery for a disc
        due to an askance sneeze
Otherwise only
hemorrhoids and you
still seem invincible to me

You talk about Vietnam
25 years later and I am
astounded to learn you were
almost killed by mortars
in the barracks tracers
on the control towers and
50 calibers in the helicopters
        after all these years
I note the sorrow in your voice
when you relate how the five
dead men looked
a trace of a tear comes
to your eye as I talk
about my younger daughter
and her miscarried brother
guardian angel

My Brother *(cont.)*

    I know you love your
son and how you want to love him
and God knows you've tried
rejection is hard
I know full well

Doris' minestrone
smooths us out
so does petting your
dogs and playing with
magnets and talking about
recipes and family and
solar panels and coelacanths

It doesn't really matter how
the world defines heroes or
invincibility because you
are my brother.

My Love
by Susan Woodfin Rogers

I do not know the where of my love -
he's sort of like the wind.
I find him often, as a wisp of cool tall shadow,
or as a sleek black feather caught in flight
among willows. My love is like the ash trees
found beside a dark green brook and I never
feel the where, the why, the when... he's often
soft in silent anger, lost somewhere between
the petals of my rose.

I know not the where of my love, he's kind of like
a smooth thought, saved away in the back of my mind.
Saved away until I can't hold back the smiles
anymore.

My love is like the morning calm. Like touches
'neath the snow.

The where my love, is never known... the hush,
and just the sigh.

My Son

And with his first breath
    His mother died.
I alone was there to hear him cry,
    He was my only child, my son.
Sarah chose his name:
    Benjamin, my son.

Red was his hair
    And green were his eyes,
Looking up at hands
    Three times his size.
First day of grade school
    I walked him there
Looking through the tears
    of pride I stared at my son.

I was his father
    His closest friend,
Now our house was blessed with two
    grown men.
At twenty he told me that he could see
    How I tried to be a family
    for my son.

Oh how I miss him here with me
Reminiscing how it used to be
Here in my hands they gave to me
Medals my boy won for bravery
My son, Oh my son.

Names

They're turning up everywhere:
familiar, forgotten names
some are working, most have quit
some in the "Who's Who"
some in the backyard gossip
most in the obit.

Timisoara, Romania

200

Nelson Mandela

When they unlatch the last bolt
and swing open the last door
the sunlight is blinding
the air is different
there is excitement and expectancy
but personal freedom is hardly an
issue after twenty-seven years.
Collective freedom is the essence.

Only now is life safe at all.
The captors of yesteryear could
be credited with saving a life,
though squelching a cause.
The incarceration of
one purposeful man
sustained it:
His example and dedication
have nurtured and fueled
it for almost three decades.

And now the work begins,
to translate personal freedom
into corporate success.

Patience has been an emotional key
    Perseverance has sustained
the physical man.
An altruistic soul
    survived the unthinkable.
For this we salute you.
Our sons and daughters salute you
and watch you be freed.
Life has no greater end
than a new beginning.

Nero

O Nero, enchant us with thy song, sweeter than a lark.
Mollify the masses with thy light touch upon the lute.
O poet of the ages, let us incline our ears to the
    verses of "Troyad."
Hold high thy garlanded head and receive thy praise.
Bread and circuses hast thou given to thy people;
Olives and grapes from the Campania hast thou given them.
Sights unseen before hast thou unveiled to thy townsmen.
Aye, hast thou also delighted in thy "Roman holidays."
How many times didst thou laugh when thou didst
    commit matricide;
When thou didst murder thy wife and brother;
When thou didst watch the conflagration of Rome
    set at thy command;
When the gladiators armed with swords, shields, nets,
    and tridents did fight to their death;
When the Christians were crucified, mangled by lions
    and Mollovian dogs, made human pillars of fire and
        used as targets by thy soldiers;
And when thou didst always place thy thumbs down?
Thou didst laugh a thousand times, a thousand times.
O thou destroyer of cities, slayer of mankind,
    and defier of the gods,
Didst not thou feel conviction, guilt, or shame?
No. Thou wast a madman without motive such as the world
        had not known.
Thou Caesar, open thy amethyst tunic and show us
    thy stone heart.
How couldst blood or even water issue from thy body?
How couldst Thanatos approach thee without trepidation?
For if not by thy will, he would not have taken you into his
    dark country.
Thy lutes, thy citharaes, shall be silent forevermore;

Nero *(cont.)*

For they perished in your eternal city with its
　　destruction.
Neither shalt thy delicate fingers strum another harp
　　for in thy death there are none.
Thy poems and lyrics also have rotted like the saffron
　　leaves upon the bloody arena.
Even if time had preserved them,
They wouldst be as the ashes of Rome before my eyes
And the smell of dead martyrs to my nostrils,
Or the thrumming of a broken lute to my ears.
Thy blood hath stained the whole world as it didst stain
　　the heather on which it fell.
The heather doth bear a bloodish flower.
The world doth bear a bloody wound.
It hath fallen.
I cover mine ears yet I hear the trickle of blood from an
innocent's heart.
I close mine eyes but I still see injustice and
　　burning cities.
I hear the heresy, the doctrines, the philosophies.
I hear the mad singing of crazed dictators.
I hear the ringing of evil.
Nero, thou didst betray thy family, thy people, thy city,
　　thy empire!
Hast thou been rewarded for thy deeds?
Yea, even to the point that thy tongue for dryness
　　cannot issue beautiful song,
　　　　　　　　　or utter a whisper.
So has it been. So is it. So shall it be.

Neutral Time

Time is no maker of friends
      man makes the friends
Time is no teller of tales
      man tells the tales
      man writes the tales
      man is the tales

Night

It was hideous
and black,
It was pitiless
and black.

Loved, revered,
Loathed and feared;
It came,
And no one knew its name,

Except I,
Who knew it had to die;
Who knew that eternity
Would be long enough
for it to go free.

Night Journey

A white moon is rising above the
stark black trees standing motionless,
silent, intent.

A wispy trail of smoke caresses them
on its ascent as the fresh snow shimmers
in mystery.

I wind my way to your light which
glimmers like the vaulted stars —

a beacon of warmth, acceptance and
security.
I stop and there is no sound; no wind.
I hate to compress such lovely adorn-
ment, but my hands are cold — and I
move onward.

San Juan Islands

Nightspeak

I hear the silent sounds of sleep
caress the night so dark and deep
Without my window 'yond my sight
Do lay the secrets of the night

Nobody speaks, no sound is heard
No flutter comes from bush or bird
And dreamy wand'rings of my mind
Do yield me all I wish to find

The passive night when no one's there
Exacts your thoughts for you to share
The darkness that doth cover me
Can only make me clearer see.

And all the world is lost in dreams
Of peace and love, a million things
That seem quite possible at night
But never do they grace the light

Upper Cataract Lake, Colorado

Nightspeak *(cont.)*

So see my friend I love this time
When all the world is hidden rhyme
When all the lanes are dew-dropped flowers
And minutes are not pawns to hours.

When all the trees are quiet maids
The shadows grow the shadows fade
And hushed songs fill the empty air
And dripping slowly linger there.

■

No one killed the albatross

No one killed the albatross
the "ancient mariner" was a psychotic.
And so was the writer
but it still made a good story.

No Regrets

I believe the greatest dilemma we face in life is
"if only", the voice of regret. The aged know well that
youth holds the key to opportunity. Why wait for
tomorrow. It's only a euphemistic never. I say, live
today and everyday until you die. No regrets.

Turnu Severin, Romania

There was a bit of moss
that etched across the sidewalk
in the late evening shadows.
The walk was cool to the touch
though the day had been warm.
There was the smell of new-mown grass
and honeysuckle and the sound
of cars on a distant busy street.
There was peace —
and pleasure in simple things
that could not be replaced.
I had taken a hard fall while jogging when I
tripped on an unlevel section of sidewalk.
I lay there almost breathless for a while;
looking up at the stars, beyond the
city lights, twinkling back at me
with answers to age-old mysteries.
I felt sorrow because I didn't know
the right questions and I felt
shame because I didn't already
know the answers.
Although I could walk
I knew I had been wounded
and - I never ran again.

Now God Let Me Forget

Forgive me if I don't call you by name...
You see, I've been to war,
And now my mind is not the same—
Since I was called afar.

Forgive me if I don't recall your face...
It's been so long, you know—
And if I don't recall the place,
Say it was long ago.

My sight's impaired by cranial wounds;
It used to be so good.
They say it may grow better soon...
O how I wish it would!

My face was burned – a mortar shell.
No hope for sweet belles now...
Well, God made man and man made hell
And war *is*, I avow.

Hi, Mother. Do you know your son?
You see, I've changed a bit.
The war is done and we have won...
O sit down, Mother, sit.

Now God Let Me Forget (cont.)

Well, now we're free and I'm back home again...
Alive... but tired and weak.
I think that all this work demands
Some food... and then some sleep.

I'll tell you all about the war someday—
Someday when you can hear...
But right now I can only pray
And you've shed many tears.

I'll tell you, when my face is healed...
Or when my thoughts are straight.
I'll tell you how my pals were killed...
But you will have to wait.

Stop crying, Mom, your son is home;
Be happy if you can.
Your boy, who's been away so long,
Has now become a man.

O thank you, God, I'm still alive...
Though Death, himself, I've met —
He left me 'til another time.
Now, God, let me forget.

O South So Dearly

O South, so dearly I love you;
So dearly were you bought —
By men in grey who took up arms
And for your region fought.

O South, so dearly I love you;
So priceless was your cost.
Your sons now lie in foreign graves
And from your care are lost.

I said the South would live again,
Would grow, and would increase,
When feet upon the mountain trail
Did bring glad news of peace.

But little did I know the South
Was torn by men in blue:
The crops were ruined, the mansions burned —
How could this thing be true?

Savannah was a terr'ble loss,
Atlanta burned in fire;
But there was more to Sherman's March
And trembling I inquired.

O South So Dearly *(cont.)*

At Vicksburg, Shiloh, they told me,
The men in grey did fall;
Eleven stars and Mother South
Did watch and cover all.

This lovely flag was tattered now
And waved on without shame
Above the bearers of her shaft
Now fallen dead or lame.

At last upon the battlefield
No smoking cannon roared.
At last the sunlight caught no gleam
From brandished gun or sword.

The rusty cannisters still lie
Upon the shell-torn field;
And there are lilies growing now
Upon the hard-won hill.

There are the graves, the shallow graves,
Marked by a cross or stone.
At Gettysburg there are the Grey
Who never made it home.

O South So Dearly *(cont.)*

My brother lies beneath a mound,
Upon his tomb a wreath,
And this dear pledge I make to him
This vow I now bequeath:

"If ever there's another war,
I for the South shall stand,"
For now she's dearer to my heart;
I love this crippled land.

Indeed, the South shall thrive again.
O yes, this land shall rise.
Her fame shall spread from East to West
And flicker through the skies.

No blockades can divert the course;
We shall amaze all eyes.
We'll build a land supreme of lands
That shall be recognized.

I never will forget the tears,
The words I heard Mom say:
"My son, should you not bear a wound?
Should you not sleep today?"

O South So Dearly *(cont.)*

And Brother as he left for war:
    "I'll see you later, Bill."
He left security of home
    To hear the bugles shrill.

Down, down the dusty road he went
    And Mother said to me
With tears, "Should you not join him
    And struggle to be free?"

I stood and watched him fade away
    Beyond the purling creek,
And saw him only once again —
    With blood-stains on his cheek.

I vow to earth and sea and sky
    That I'll defend my home;
That I shall never falter when
    The cavalry's coming on.

O brother! Brother! Woe is me.
    What has this coward done?
O why should I be living when
    You are the gallant one.

O South So Dearly (cont.)

O fate! O fate! Give me a chance
At fighting such as this.
Red badge of courage, you I want;
If I could have, what bliss!

The tattered flag has long been furled,
A fruitless fight is o'er.
One banner waves up in the sky
And peace from shore to shore.

The emblem of the South still flies
Within my fervent heart;
And hidden memories through my mind
Do come and then depart:

My mother's words, my brother's face,
The battlefields so quiet,
The lateness of my visiting them,
And tales of bloody fights.

I see the crops, the cities grow,
The rivers deep and wide,
The mountains, plains, and forests green,
And I am filled with pride.

O South So Dearly *(cont.)*

I hear the horn of riverboats,
The friendly speech of all,
The singing birds, the willow's sigh,
A cow-horn's lonely call.

I smell the sweet gardenia flow'rs,
The oats inside the barn,
Magnolia blossoms in the Spring
And fresh hay on the farm.

I taste the savory smokehouse hams,
And sweet potato pie,
The ripe dewberries from the vine
And chicken golden-fried.

And all of these are of the South
And of the South alone.
The dearest sights, the sweetest sounds,
Are all about my home.

O South, so dearly I love you;
So dearly were you bought ——
By men in grey who took up arms
And for your region fought.

O South So Dearly (cont.)

O South, so dearly we love you;
But, O, what was the cost?
Some sons now sleep in foreign fields
And from your care are lost.

And may those men who died away,
From Mother South's sweet care,
Be solaced by some southern winds
While they are sleeping there.

Fordyce, Arkansas

Obsession and Compulsion

Your smile was in the trees
Your eyes in the sky
Your hands in the wind
Your voice in the rain
Your soul in the sidewalk
And just as meaningless as time
          and just as deep as the universe's shoes
I shall rise up to the belt buckle of hope
and cram my petition in your navel
"Come out you holy whore! Come out
wherever you are!
The bed is ready for your wiles
and I **have my last penny**".

Ocean City, MD

As day yields to night
you take my hand
and along the beach
we walk into the sun.

As dusk yields to night
you take my hand
the sea at our feet
we walk into the sun.

In the scarlet dusk
you take my hand
the sea is begging at our feet
we walk into the sun.

Of One

Were there words that could express
what my mind tries to repress
I could tell you friend or foe
light and darkness you would know.

But no words my tongue can tell
since those last few phrases fell
Fell upon an ear of one
who saw not the morning sun.

And I saw while standing there
all the evergreens were bare
And gazing at the greying sky
I felt tears fill up my eye.

Of This Is A Man
A Fifteen-year-old's Perspective
Dedicated to the late President, John F. Kennedy

One who can stand up and proudly say,
"I am a man" — is all of this:
He that is judged by what he is,
Not as he looks;
What he does,
Not what he says he will do;
Always trying to attain greater heights,
But never forgetting the ones who
    helped him attain those heights;
Always walking with kingly pride,
But common enough too.
This man should think,
For thought is a great master.
Then with this idea,
He should put his hands, body, and heart to work.
Then with this creation,
Whether of rock, pen and paper, or canvas and paints,
It will be his and possibly he will attain these
    greater heights——
And respecting, cherishing, and working for the
            better things,
He will succeed.
Luxury will be his.
Importance will he have.
Famed will he be.

Of This Is A Man (cont.)

A million tongues will exalt him!
A million hands shall hold him high!
Through triumph and disaster,
He will be backed by these millions.
Then as time goes by ———
And this man has served his term, his people,
      his country,
This man shall pass away
To the glory beyond the skies.
The millions shall mourn
And each one will think of him,
Who for them did die,
A martyr for mankind and this ugly world.
But fear not for him
Nor shed a single tear,
For this man has gone to glory, The Promised Land!
And there will he receive his rewards
For the mighty works that he did do
On this earth.
But do not forget him!
No, he will not be forgotten.
Though he lies still in the wooden box,
He will live on ———
In the hearts of those he helped,
His country will not forget him.
His name will be proclaimed

Of This Is A Man (cont.)

From North to South and East to West.
And the Red and White and Blue will be flown at
    half-mast for him.
To it was he loyal.
He tried to make his country pure
And shed his blood for her.
Yes, this man attained the greater heights.

This man gained fame.
This man was praised.
He served his country well.
This was a man.

Old Glory of 1870

Flying, folding, flowing, furling,
Yes, I've watched that banner waving,
Pure and lovely, warm and saving,
O'er the thousands who were raving,
Above a disunited land.
Men in Blue the conflict braving,
Freeing those who had been slaving,
Pleasing those who had been craving
To see that banner whole again.

Flowing ever gently, smoothly,
Let it hang there now and ever,
Let no traitor's sword dissever
That which we shall love forever,
Now as one nation evermore.
Let it hold this land together,
Though the clouds of conflicts gather,
Floating lightly as a feather,
To be dissevered nevermore.

Old Glory of 1870 (cont.)

Watch it waving, floating, furling,
In the sunlight proudly streaming,
With its colors grand and gleaming,
And to some it has the seeming
Of an emblem that's divine.
O'er the thousands that are teeming,
Looking, loving, hoping, dreaming,
With its splendor it is beaming
In this happy heart of mine.

Watch it flying, folding softly,
O'er expanses of the nation,
Winning there a grand ovation,
Let it face no degradation,
O, let it fly forever free.
For it has been liberation,
And it has been our salvation,
Let there be no derogation,
O, let it wave where we can see.

Old Glory of 1870 (cont.)

Flowing ever lightly, lovely,
While the children now are singing
To the flag and bells are ringing,
And the birds above are winging,
Around this banner in the sky.
And all eyes to it are clinging,
And the people's hearts are tingling,
And these happy souls are mingling
Beneath the flag, O let it fly!

Old Slewfoot

Old slewfoot slips up
to steal your lifeblood
You think you can handle it
but it's no good.

He's choking at your throat
and sucking your blood out.
You will not have victory
if paralyzed by doubt.

He's torching all your lifeblood
with a ruthless cutting arc;
and once that he has flamed you out
you're headed for the dark.

You'll be dead, defeated,
a part of history;
spiritually dead, unneeded,
in abject poverty —
If you don't have the courage to stand,
you will fall.
If you aren't faithful to the Lord,
You will lose all.
You will lose all.
If you aren't faithful to the Lord
you will lose all.

Once you had a chance
to let your light shine
but you covered it up
for some other time.

Old Slewfoot *(cont.)*

You think that you can live
on both sides of the street.
You try to hedge your bets
to never see defeat.

But now you finally know:
It's time to pay your dues;
the Man's walking down the hall.
There's one last chance to choose.

Or be dead, defeated,
a part of history;
spiritually dead, unneeded,
in abject poverty —
If you don't have the courage to stand,
you will fall.
If you aren't faithful to the Lord,
You will lose all.
You will lose all.
If you aren't faithful to the Lord
you will lose all.

You think the road of life should be
an easy downhill course;
You never have believed the Word:
We've got to take the world by force!
You've sailed atop a crystal lake
in your naievete,
but you're coming to a waterfall;
It's the end you cannot see.

Old Slewfoot *(cont.)*

You'll be dead, defeated,
a part of history;
spiritually dead, unneeded,
in abject poverty —
If you don't have the courage to
stand,
you will fall.
If you aren't faithful to the Lord,
You will lose all.
You will lose all.
If you aren't faithful to the Lord
you will lose all.

San Diego Zoo, California

On Leaving Chicago
2-22-92

You exhibit that embarrassing vulnerability; go way beyond
congeniality; offer encouraging overtures; and then a few
days later you have 180°'d on me. It's like we are hardly
acquaintances anymore. Everything becomes purely technical, if we talk at all.

I frankly get puzzled, realize it's your prerogative and doubt
that you're trying to be cruel.

I believe there are a lot of memories and people that get in
the way of your love; and some people will selfishly cling to
you with the deception that they are trying to protect you.
The fact is, they need you more than you need them. There
was a time you needed them very much, but no longer.

No one can (and no one should) tell you what to do. Knowing you, I would think that fear and scare tactics would drive
you in the opposite direction of what a person proposes. You
can still listen and entertain the options.

Basically, I believe, this mid-life stuff is a search for spiritual
significance. It's good we came to this point; and better now
then later. If the root problem is spiritual, it behooves us to
address that primarily.

I'm looking at the rivets in an airplane wing. Your memories, bad and good, are as solidly driven in as those rivets.
They are undeniable. They resist change in the conformation
of the wing just like your memories resist the notion of
change in me.

I don't blame you for doubting. However, maybe your fear
that I have changed is more bothersome. Only you could
really know. Are you afraid to know?

233

On Loving Again

A cascade of purple smoke finds my broken heart in the
early morning. The promise of warmth propels me
on in the bitter cold of sad memories and broken
dreams. The ice is not even broken in the ditches.
The sunrise timidly peeks over the black hills, framed
in hope, cautiously eager to awaken the sleeping passions,
erase the hangovers of bitterness, dispel the sorrows of
ignorance and error.

I find my footsteps quickening though my hands and feet
are numb. I *will* see and hear the warm breath of compassion, the sweet sounds of life in the dead of morning, a
smoke signal of help in the frosty air.

I will deny that I can feel it though it is thawing out my
rejected soul, drawing it to the surface again, dismantling
the trappings of hibernation.

And so I come to this place, and the spring suns on a
thousand tundras would not feel as majestic: cancelling
winter, calling out courageous tendrils to reach for the sky.
The deepest purple gives way to gold and orange – and for a
moment, the past becomes a stranger cloaked in anonymity
skirting down a dim, back street.

I never thought that I would stand here again by design.
I do not want an opiate. I want to feel the pain - but not
forever.

Sometimes I am fearful that I will. Sometimes I feel that
I've felt enough for this life and the next. You answer my
knock and you know.

You know that rivers and canyons and mountains
and prairies and lakes and tall trees and pine forests and
gulches and deserts lie between us. You sense a feeling of
awe as I do that we can stand here face to face.

My mind is speeding down a water chute, a double
diamond downhill; behind a ski boat with all its centrifugal
forces.

On Loving Again *(cont.)*

    You are steady, poised, expectant. Static prickles the air, waiting for some interruption, some extraneous exposé of our legerdemain: a phone ring, water dripping, a child's needs.
    You answer before I can even ask a question and it frankly scares me. It scares me to think I've been wrong about myself or that you could be wrong and not know it. Maybe I have just changed. Maybe I was never bad. I just don't know.
    Your energy snaps me back while an incandescent bulb beams an eidetic image that obscures your face momentarily.
    You are holding me without hands. You are kissing me without lips. You are guiding me inside you without touching.
My mind reels like some rabbit chased by the beagles, circling back toward the hunters again; like the approach-avoidance emotions that well up in me when I hear the sound of white water approaching.
    The ferris wheel stops just forward from its zenith and swings slightly back and forth, to and fro. Change and chapstick roll out on the seat in which I'm placidly suspended. The smell of cotton candy reaches up to me and *you bridge the gap*.

On Return

It was good t' be home.
Mother said she was bakin' my favorite pie:
apple. And as I sat
I thought bout the places I'd been
and the things I'd seen
since I last was home
and I thought bout when I was a child
how I couldn't reach the sink
t' wash my hands
and now how I had t' bend
way over t' touch it
and then how I could stand straight 'n tall
but now as a man I had t' stoop
t' what others say
and I thought bout the things
I'd always accepted without a thought
as true and now how they
seemed like a lie
like they used t' say
"If we're goin' t' have peace
we got t' always be fightin' for it"
and you know one day I stopped
and said t' myself if we're always in war
fightin' for peace how in the hell
are we gonna ever have it
and sometimes I want t' say
"Kill me world fore hate of peace does"
and as I sat there Mother talked
bout people I couldn't remember
but what scared me was I didn't care any
so I just nodded my head like I was hearin'

and I tried t' smile but I couldn't
cause I couldn't laugh cause I couldn't cry
cause I couldn't care.
I looked out the window
and saw a new house. Several.
And it made me feel better
cause I knew those people were gettin' rich
and didn't care any either.
Of course I wasn't exactly like them
cause I was poor but that was good
cause it meant I had less t' worry bout.
Yes it was good t' be home awhile
even though it was a dump.
It was good t' hear Mother talk,
t' hear how stupid people are
and sittin' and thinkin'
and then just sittin'
I decided I didn't like apple pie no more.

On Return II

I was rambling down the same familiar road in a huge
yellow Suburban Boger had lent me. Going back to my
roots. The population had dropped 100 and things looked
about the same except for the new school. The hunting
woods were all cut away to make room for rice and wheat,
and you could see the levee all the way to Potluck - about 8
or 9 miles.

Issues of 20 years ago resurfaced when my mom talked
about "the nigra" who did this or that.

Turnip greens and turnips and cornbread were the delicious meal along with sweetened tea.

A black gentleman had been contracted to fix the sagging
carport for $25.00. Rotten boards and sheets of bent tin
faced him. My mother also wanted rolls of felt-type lining
put between the tin and the support structure. Also tar. I
wondered whether the black man had any qualms as we
opened the can of tar to make sure it was still liquid. It was a
day's work in the cold. My mother also remarked that he got
tar all over his clothes. It looked like a good job and she
haplessly pulled her car under the restored port to find
(somewhat later) conspicuous black dribbles of fresh tar all
over the car.

Conversation addressed issues of family members: A
new husband for my sister; a new job for my brother; a
needed occupational direction for a nephew; emotional
problems of a niece, etc. We touched on religion and the
often perfunctory nature of worship. Political issues were
submerged by rehabilitation from orthopedic injuries, the
turnip green crop, changing out new-used bed springs,
neighborhood illnesses, and questions about my family.
We went to see Aunt Maude. The house was dark in the
twilight. She came to the door and asked us in. The kitchen
was very dimly illuminated by the rays of setting sun.

On Return II (cont.)

A small wrapped present and a sack of pecans completed the
Christmas exchange. The conversation went on while we
awkwardly stood. The kitchen was tidy but very simple and
old. I finally sat down and her huge cat came in cautiously
to investigate. The octagenarian spoke about her health -
three cancer operations over the years - and how she thought
the lump was coming back in her belly. But she was not
going to do anything 'this' time - she was 88. God had given
her a long life. I had not seen her in 20 years and left
knowing I would not see her again.

On Seeing the Unmailed Letter
by Bart Pullen

Setting on the worn window sill,

What mystery is there standing still?

Whose fate does it bear?

And what great loss for whom no one cares?

For if someone cared

This shadow could no longer stare.

What is in this cobweb invested

Which some soul has rested till rusted?

This great mystery the eyes do see

Is still sealed in the envelope before me.

One Cannot Escape

One cannot escape the reality of God.
His contribution becomes evident
in our successes and his comforting
presence in the midst of our failures.

I turn to him with praise when life is grand
and prayers when it is hard to understand.
During mundane times and mediocrity,
I can transcend to abundancy and eternity.

Blue Ridge Parkway

One of the Strangest Things

This is going to be one of the strangest things
of your life
This is going to be one of the strangest things
of your life
Under the rainbow tree
Where love is free
A naked father cries
clasping his rosary
One of the strangest things
in his life.

This is going to be one of the strangest things
of your life
This is going to be one of the strangest things
of your life
Inside the outer world
Where clouds are furled
in iridescent skies
a sign says "think of me"
One of the strangest things
in your life.

This is going to be one of the strangest things
of your life
This is going to be one of the strangest things
of your life

We heard the morning smile
And ran to be its child
before it died
But time had stopped to see
One of the strangest things
in our life.
This is going to be one of the strangest things
of your life
This is going to be one of the strangest things
of your life
Don't try to understand
just take my hand
and please don't wonder why
Just like a bird on wings
One of the strangest things

This is going to be one of the strangest things
of your life
This is going to be one of the strangest things
of your life
Don't lose yourself in words
that are not heard
Please look into my eyes
Just like an humble king
One of the strangest things.

Only Yesterday

I carried toys yesterday
In gentle hands as I did play
And stubby fingers left a trail
in sands where all my dreams did sail

I rubbed my eyes to clear the tears
That had emerged from childish fears
And felt sweet words and helping hands
That understood my least demands.

But now today it is not then
My first beginnings are at end
And now my fingers one by one
Have laced themselves around a gun.

My eyes have tears within them yet
They cry with hate and yet regret
And worlds once bended to my will
Have grasped my throat and wait to kill!

Our Love
by Susan Woodfin Rogers

love is like the winds that blow – a free
uncaptured thing.
love is like the coffee sting of birds caught by
the sky. love is almost knowing all the clouds,
to call them one by one. love is like a breaded-
leaf with earth's small knowledge kept inside.
winter comes in snow. and spring with flowers
that are sweet. and summer talks with laughing
hearts of things to do and see.
but our love is like the autumn winds...
a thing – like you and me

Waterfall, Tuscon, Arizona

Our Time
(To Susan -- Eleven years later)

The Summer is clutching for its life
and the relentless cold rain is thwarting its efforts ---

There's a certain smell in the air,
    a certain feel
        a preface,
            a prelude,
                a foreword
                    a maybe-breath of
Fall —

                        perhaps.
It's just a brief matter of time until
    cool nights and
        bright stars
            and vivid moons and
                tawny sunsets and
                    fog at dusk and
                        frost on
surprised grass.

        It won't be long until I'll say again,
        I love you,
        and mean it more
        than ever before —
        Love is a natural concomitant
        of Autumn:
        Toes seem to find
        one another more easily before
        dancing fireplaces;
        over tall cups of coffee

sweetened with brown sugar;
beneath heavy quilts
handed down from great-grandmothers;
in aromatic rustling leaves.
You touch your cheek
in fleeting thought,
in momentary passion,
in melancholic wistfulness,
in anticipation.
You almost say it,
mouth half-open
but then turn away
quickly, knowing
to mention it doesn't help.

It's a time when everything
is dying, but lovers
(who are blooming).
We always come back to it;
though it takes longer
some years than others —
there have been some
very long years:
Endless days
frayed and shriveled by heat,
intimidated by the face-to-face
stare of a 100 watt
bulb and a buzzing fly
screaming frantically
in its death-swoon;
by the startling cry of a cricket-

intruder; by the dry languid
silence of lifeless nights
and the semi-embarrassment
of blinding mornings.

Heat and sweat and waiting
put years on a man:
squint-lines on his face, a
retreating hairline,
a loss of form.

It's an ice cream truck
making a lightning
run by the seaside
for little children
with burning feet,
clutching funny-
money in
their sweaty palms,
dirt in the creases,
beads of sweat on their noses;
this is their day.
It's the disruptive whirr
of a power mower on
Sunday morning by
the pot-bellied retired army sergeant
with a crewcut,
a turquoise & red
Vietnamese lady on one deltoid,
"Mother" on the
other & "sweet" and "sour" nipples.

Our Time *(cont.)*

It's the hot battleship
grey oppressive smoke
of the industrial
district, the incessant
whine of the power
station, the stifling
death-scent of the
5 o'clock exhaust,
the frightening furor
of mad trucks
with suffering brakes,
the muffled cry of
the 60-year-old newspaper
huckster with unshaven
face, dirty underwear
and a bottle of
whiskey in the back
pocket of his sagging
pants. (His
suspenders hold his
life in some
semblance of order).

It's the dispassionate
out-of-the-corner-of-his-cigar
smile of the porno-man,
sometimes wondering
whether he has contributed
to the greater bad
of mankind: the rapist,
the fornicator, a

divorce, a death, an
attitude. He knows he has.

It's the haunting
wail of sirens in the
dead of night:
a death or near-death
of something or someone;
perhaps, an after-the-fact
futile epithet.

It's the vomit on the
street the day after,
replete with green flies,
from the chaotic
stomach of a man
who hates himself
& his own,
an unwillful but
inevitable
usurper of a life
or spirit.
It's the depressing
sight of distant lightning
in a sultry sky (you
know rain will never materialize);
the putrid stench of watermelon
rinds and one-week-old
fish heads;
the forlorn sound of
tractors tilling in the

Our Time (cont.)

night and tugs passing
on the river; the
vociferocity of the old
courthouse clock rigidly
tolling the early morning
hours as you lie
awake, awaiting the
return of a persistent
mosquito; the
deafening croak of
big bullfrogs just over
the levee in barpits
hosting cottonmouth
moccasins; the smell
of dust in the nostrils;
the solemn
thud of a ripe pear
obeying gravity;

the endless repertoire of
a mockingbird insomniac,
profaning Christmas carols
in August;
the dismaying pilgrimage of all the
six-leggers and eight-leggers
convening for a handout.

Our Time (cont.)

I love you most
in October, November,
the Autumn
when the hillsides are ignited with
magnificent hues and
friendly puffs of cool air
bring smells of fresh
mown hay,
a recent skunk, the
cow pasture, an
oak log
giving up its soul,
burgundy brambles
sheltering cottontails,
ham frying in the skillet.

September is about
to fade into October,
again,
It took so long.
How many years older
did we get this year?
Your hand is on mine,
your eyes serene,
understanding;
eagerly awaiting our
time, the time for
lovers.
It won't be long
until I'll say again,
I love you
and mean it more than ever before.

Playing Golf

Playing golf is immoral for me because it's so addicting. It's like an alcoholic who doesn't have the alcohol dehydrogenase enzyme and gets hooked, or something like that.

I liked the danger of golf, the heady fear of hooking or slicing into the other fairway and hitting someone. The instant crouch and hail Mary whenever you hear "Fore"; standing anywhere on the tee with any of my friends when they (try to) tee off. Those balls are small but they hurt. I love it in the fall when every sane person had gone to War Memorial Stadium to watch Razorback football. You could pretend that the cheers were for your great chip shot with no less a 7 iron rather than a pitching wedge; or did you see that 20 ft. putt or near-hole-in-one?

A long drive ranks right up there with good sex and holy spirit anointing, but a topped ball is the worse: keplunk, keplunk, plunk. The harder you try, the worse it gets.

The most balls I ever remember losing were 12 in 18 holes. I was playing alone (that really shows you're addicted) and lost half of the balls in the sun (such fastastic drives! Skyballs?) The other half-dozen I lost trying to hit over a water trap. Water has a + charge and golf balls have - charges I found out.

It's amazing I ever shot in the 90's (or the high 80's with a little cheating in the rough). I remember bolting out of neuroanatomy and physiology tests ASAP to make it to the golf links. That may explain why neuro was one of my least glamorous academic achievements; because I was playing so much golf is maybe because of this subject.

In any event, I will never forget hitting over the hill on 15 to the green; and hookin on the 18th tee into unwary traffic on Markham Street. I still have the left-handed clubs I bought from Johnny Hearnsberger for $30.00 in 1973. Those babies are old and they're all the clubs I have.

Playing Golf (cont.)

I was given a box of Titlest balls 2 years ago and they're still unopened. I keep eyeing them. Someone talked about playing golf a few weeks back and I got real excited.
I thought I would have to get some of the dust and cobwebs off the golf bag, etc. However, the plans didn't work out.
I was kinda glad, actually, cause I have all this stuff I need/want to do and a fun golf game would blow it out the window.

I don't think I could just be a social golfer, so I will have to avoid it for a few more years. Play racketball, tennis, run, etc. and not partake of golf for awhile yet.

Mount Washington Hotel, New Hampshire

Postlude of Destruction

O taste the fruits of victory:
　　The ashes and the fire.
So long mad leaders craved this day;
　　fulfilled is their desire.

The end, the end, how true it came,
　　unfaltering and sure;
Yet when a fire sweeps o'er a land,
　　It leaves it black but pure.

White Mountains, New Hampshire

Pringlish
with Ken Helton

In ye gay ole London town
Everyone doth wear a frown
While the dew drops softly down
Upon the hot and arid ground.

Choirs are singing late tonight
While the sun is burning bright
Everyone is snuggled tight
In empty beds ... that sounds right

Everyone is on their feet
Cars are racing down the street
People stifled by the heat
Fall frozen then upon their seats.

Progress

The fire burns low beneath the hearth;
A thousand years have come and gone
And though I've met a million friends
I now sit here alone.
For when the churches ceased to pray
And courts to look for proof
And God was put on dollar bills
I still held on to truth.
And so the world has left me here
To search for what they will not find
For things they do may be called right
But I still have a mind.
So I sit here and nod my head
Too old for a new start.
That hearth of mine is stars above;
The dying fire, my heart.

Propriety

Because of your beguiling manner and because I hold those
people closest whom I have never known, I send you
this token of my imagination to share in the weakest hour
of your thoughts and the finest hour of your dreams.

I ask to be your friend, who can be no more.
So tragic that we should constrain our life to one room
with no escape,
to hear the hollow sound of our echoing voice
against the wall of our loneliness.
        Why is everything so simple?

Why can't we have reasons, and rationalizations, and why's?
    We only have fear.   Squandered by our own minds
we hide in our shell of external complacency:
        yearning,
        searching,
        aching,
        dying.

Reaching out with our hands but running with our
    feet. Running away -- from everything we desire.
Our voice speaks but our ears are quick to
obscure the answer.
        It is this way.
        This is the way I am.
        Probably the way you are.
But more tragic, is not that we are this way,
but that this is the way we will continue to be.

Reason

"The eye opens into darkness:
In the realm of forgetfulness,
In the interludes of forced existence.
It espies reason without description,
Knowledge without conveyance,
Logic without premise.

The ear opens into silence:
To the deafening roar of being,
To persistent throb of heartbeats
Spanning the gulf between what is
and what could be;
Between what we are (will) and
What we wish (would).

Each man learns to face himself with tears
No matter how many stand to wipe his eyes
And soothe his ears,
For seeing is in perceiving,
And hearing is in interpreting,
And existence has no meaning without ...."

"But," interrupted Socrates,
"what if the world be elliptical?"

Reconciliation

You were drifting away from me
and I couldn't bring you back
It was like a dark fantasy
I couldn't face the facts
We were drifting apart somehow
and I didn't know why
But finally we drifted back
With love and a sigh.

With love and a sigh
With love and a sigh
Our feet on the earth
Our heads in the sky
With love and a sigh
With love and a sigh
We turned and we met
With love and a sigh.

Red Tape

If I were such a man
I would be more than a man
I would be a god
on the universal comode
and every problem
I desired not to face
I
would
flush.
And I would sit
with good measure
on my solid rump
and be common enough
to hear any good man out.
For it is written
"He who hears the
common man must hear
the uncommon man
for parrots are
to puppets king."

Refuge

The door is a thick one
and the knock is muffled - but heard
You whisper – appropriate reverence
for such a night
Your hands are warmer
than ever
The fireplace draws me with
irresistible magnetism
and I stand in peace –
rewarded, consoled, soothed.
You are so warm –
untouched by the night
The covers are heavy and warm
the room is densely black
and spinning as our thoughts
blend, diffuse and melt into sleep
The last thing I can ever
remember is the *roar* of silence.

Rehabilitation - 1965
(to my high school principal)

With DLO
the word was "go"
And many left in sorrow
To shear their locks
And don their socks
And come to school the morrow.

So back they came
With tears and shame
for all their heads were peeled
And now you see
identities
of many were revealed.

Resolution

January translates all our loneliness
into new expectations,
and overstriving for happiness
contrives our being
to an extent that the end is elusive.

Freud and all the king's men
can't put our fractured egos
back together again;
much less give them back to the
rightful owners.

Retreat
(Crow's Nest, Grey Gull Inn 1980 - Wells, Maine)

Nothing but the rolling waves touching an
unconcerned coastline outside —

A seal mounts a dark grey rock to gather some
early morning sun. The world here is quiet and grey –
and largely asleep as are you. It's good to have time to
be nobody, to retreat, regroup and revitalize. It's good
to rest without interruption and upcoming obligation;
and that is to say, truly to rest.

There is something mysterious about isolation -
almost forbidden, almost surrealistic.

Here there are echoes of the past: steep stairways,
a maze of rooms, muffled voices; and vivid imaginations to entertain the empty mind.

There is time to eat, sleep, love and dream —
and particularly, to dream.

Revelation
(1320 Southedge, Little Rock,1979)

I ask you if you love me;
You say you *did*.
How long ago? **Silence**.
    Some time before the side of my bed
was perennially empty
and the lamp at my desk
burned on past midnight--
Mystifying affinitive bugs and
usurping the glory of fireflies,
Casting dancing shadows on an
overgrown lawn, displaying an unriveted
swingset. Despite the chill of October winds
unwary wasps still cling to tenacious nests
constructed at the outset of summer
in the playhouse no longer frequented.
A large grey nest of yellow-jackets
hangs among the dying tomato vines -
and even the dogs are aware of forbidden places.
    Some time before I stopped talking
about work and dreams and being famous
and going places and doing things and
seeing friends and going to church and
what the kids did yesterday.
    Some time before I stopped kissing you on your
zygomatic and the side of your neck and holding you
tightly and rubbing your back and holding your hand
and kissing your back and massaging your feet.
    Some time before "I love you" (because I never stopped
saying it) became an amenity, a salutation without physical
expression or intellectual concern.
    Some time before journals became my mistresses, before
nights of physical exercise habitually separated us.

Rushes Green for
What They're Worth

Rushes green
Along the shore
Have been
But shall be nevermore.

Birds with song
Who soar so high
Have long refused
To grace this sky.

Stately swans
who love the lakes
and ponds,
Shall never know these brakes.

And men who hold
to yesterday
Must weep
the happy world away.

Sassafras and Cedar

Sassafras and cedar
Willows by the score
Rustling cottonwoods
and stately sycamores
Sweet wysteria
and chinaberries too
Honeysuckle
bathed in dew —

You burst on the scene my love,
beauty Nature can't afford.
Tawny sunsets bow and rainbows
    grace the sky
nature cheers in one accord.

Butterbeans and okra
Cantaloupe and corn
Sweet banana peppers
gourds that adorn
Bright red tomatoes
Clinging to the vine
Purple egg-
plants that shine.

You burst on the scene my love,
beauty Nature can't afford.
Tawny sunsets bow and rainbows
    grace the sky
nature cheers in one accord.

Satisfaction

I wish my epitaph to be
"If you look here you won't find me."
Another thing I ask of ye:
There on my grave don't plant a tree.

I want a box and that is all,
A simple box with sturdy walls
So if the worms begin to gnaw,
No one into my grave will fall.

I am a cordial sort of man
But I'm afraid I'd have no hand;
And too I'm sure they'd need a fan
And prob'ly not come back again.

So if a casket make it good,
With velvet and with cedar wood.
Then paint it purple if *you* would
For I do not think that *I* could.

And if I have a choice of shrouds,
O let it be one long and loud
So I'll be noticed if somehow
I do wake up beyond the clouds.

O put me down about four feet,
Not quite too shallow or too deep.
And if these promises ye'll keep,
I shall not wake up in my sleep.

Shadows and Windows

Shadows of night
And windows of light
Shine from my valley
So clear and so bright

Whispers of laughter
And words of the wind
Wind through my valley
And sound without end

Echo and echo
Down paths lined with peace
May they e'er be with me
May they never cease.

May love and good fortune
Be ever with you
May God bless your valley
And my valley too.

She Slipped Away

She slipped away like the tide,
like a sunset, like childhood,
and left me waiting for the past.
I see her footprints in my mind
and run to follow with my thoughts,
but there are places where even
my fantasies cannot go.

Three Mile Beach, Washington

Shells

small things white things
soft within the Hand
grey wings swift wings
high above the sand

I am you are
yes we all are now
so far too far
wish our heads could bow

can't find there aren't
shells upon the sand
today each day
now inside the Hand

one time some time
fragile bones remained
once yes East West
nothing now is gained

all now same now
none are White or Red
sleep deep so deep
all the beach is dead

on the in the
Hand yes in the Hand
so tired too tired
now to understand

Shoes

Tramp, tramp, poor shoes
Snug beneath my feet
Clomp, clomp, clomp, clomp
Hear the steady beat.

Scrape! Scrape, poor soles
On the sultry walk
Squeak, squeak, squeak, squeak
Listen to them talk.

Wiggle, wiggle, big toe
High above the street
Clickety clack, clickety clack
Hear the taps repeat.

Rest, rest, tired shoes
Street light up ahead
Soon the slippers will be on
And you can go to bed.

Shotguns and Sequins

some naive,
some prude, some lewd
some hot, some not
some cold, some old
some fun, some none
some cut, and some pure
some sure, and some not so sure
some hope, some grope
some wait 9 months
some only wait 4

Stratford, Oklahoma

274

Significants

Who cares if one cried?
It was just a head of hair
And I will probably lose it anyway.
So why not conform?:
Shave my head!
If I lose a love for cutting my hair,
She wasn't much of a love anyway.
There, better.
Now I look like all the others:
Railroad tie number two billion 239
or serial number blah, blah, blah.
We are just numbers anyway
So why not cut my hair?
Who should care but I
About myself?

Significants

Time always finds me sitting on my doorstep
Wondering what happened to the years:
The day we landed on the moon
Ten thousand starved to death in India
A young man burned his last year's
           classification card
While a monk burned himself.
And we all laughed with our shaven heads,
With ripples of laughter running across
           our fat bellies.
With stubby fingers I reached out
For another chocolate
As the news commentator announced
That God had unconditionally succumbed.
           And communism had gone to hell
And everything else had generally
Gone to pot.
           And in remembrance
I pulled out a dollar bill one more time
Just to remember what God looked like
And I giggled
Because God had his head shaved!
           And it was so funny
I threw up formula
All over my houseshoes.

Significants (cont.)

I must take a walk
To find a part of myself I have lost.
The sun isn't shining
But I'll decide to live anyway.

So Close

You're so close now
I can almost touch you,
or, at least, watch you sleep
Dreaming of me
and times gone by —
or to come.
Still making me a hero
beyond laughter or applause
Still the man of the hour
though often two hours late.
Still patient and kind
despite all my unkindness
Still understanding
despite my confusion.
Always smoothing me out,
nestling me down
rounding me out.

So Dies the Heart
by Ken Helton

As the tiny sparrow dies,
So dies the heart;
On wings of guileless life
Toward death depart

Dust-brown, in the twilight time
The sparrow flits,
Thinking still that day's bright strength
About him sits

In this way the foolish heart
Flees from fearing
Hoping that the faded light
Is sunrise nearing

Sodoman

You've all heard the story of Sodoman - you know, the
guy who had 300 wives and 700 combines. Now this king
wasn't like his daddy David - he's the one who was always
chasing philipines and getting in bar-room brawls with guys
bigger'n him. His daddy was different 'cause he only had
one or two wives at the time. You see, Sodoman was wise
and good and supraintelligent. He was straighter than most
(Israelite) rulers. David, you know, was the one who killed a
giant philipine called -- a lot of names. This giant was a
malignant sight. His biceps and other muscles budged out.
And this small David with only a dollar-store slingshot and
three rocks killed Galiath.

I would evaporate further on the subject, but time doesn't
permit me. Back to Sodoman. He had fearful courage like
his father, who stole his mother from her bath and so named
her bathsheeba. The other part of her name, Shoeba, came
from her family town of Beersheeba. Her father was named
Maltsheba, her mother Slitzsheba, and her brother Budsheba.
Anyway, back to the story of Sodoman. One day he was
walking down the Roman Superhighway when he was met
by 3,000 philipines. Can you believe that? 3,000 philipines
with 400 chariots. Would you believe 300 philipines and 20
chariots? Would you believe one old woman on a mule?
Anyway, the philipines attacked from every side, top, and
bottom. Undented, Sodoman stood. Like the rock of
Gibralter, like the Eiffel Tower, like the leaning tower of
Pizza. You know that's the building that Leonardo de Vinci
dropped a lump of dough off and killed a man. By chance,
he saw the skeleton of a zebra hidden in the sand. Quickly
he seized a jawbone to defend himself with. Then came the
onslop of the philipines. They came with a terrible din, and a
lot of hollering too. And there stood Sodoman with the
jawbone branquished above his head and his tanned body

glistering in the sun. His face tensioned, his mouth was set,
his eyes burned like fire, his eyebrow twitched. His chest
expanded, his biceps and triceps flexed, his thighs tightened,
his calf muscle hardened, his little toe itched.

Just then he looked at his sundial and realized he was late
for his date with Deliar, so he threw the jawbone at the
philipines and ran. It so happened that he threw the zebra
jawbone so hard that it kept bouncing up and down and all
around til it killed every philipine and cut down every tree in
the valley. Today it is appropriately name Death Valley.

Now Diliar was a beautiful woman whose hair was wavy,
whose eyelashes were wavy, whose figure was wavy too.
But she was a philipine.

Now Diliar wished to know the source of Sodoman's
strength so that she might destroy him. So she asked him,
"My dear cutie, where do you get such strength?"
Neverthemore, Sodoman was very prudent. He was also a
very wise man. So he said, " I get my strength from vitamins." It was arranged that he couldn't have any vitamins.
Neverthemore, in the proceeding week he split the Goradian
knot. So Deliar asked him again,"Sodoman, what is the
source of your strength?" Now Sodoman was a very ingenu-
ous man, so he kept his secret by telling her sunflower seeds
were his source of power. She saw to that it he could not eat
such food. Howevermore, the next week he performed a
splendifferent feat. He held his hand against a hole in a dike
and kept the Dead Sea from flooding Mecca. Yet, as strong
as he was, Sodoman weakened to Deliar's pleading. He told
her he hadn't gotten a haircut since he was born. He told her
he must have had one then because his mother told him he
was bald. "So, it is his hair that gives him strength!" As
wise as Sodoman was wise, he couldn't read. This
probably can be attributed to the fact that he didn't go

beyond the first grade. They expulsed him for his long hair
style. Hereuntofore, when Deliar gave him some sleeping
pills he didn't know what they were. Being real hungry he
ate the whole bottle. He slept for twenty years —— No that's
another story. While he slept Deliar cut off the locks from
his head; she also cut off his hair. When he awoke he was
bounded with locks and chains. He tried to break his bind-
ings but he could not. So he cried out and he also spoke, "I
can't free myself!" Then with inquisitive laughter Deliar
dispersed a mirror before him. Much was his depression and
sadity, for he looked like the philipine king, Yul Brimmer.
"Take the mirror away or either punch out my eyes!" So
they did both. The philipines took Sodoman and placed him
in prison. Blinded and weak in prison, he felt the burning
desire to expressify himself in words. So he hired the
services of a young man called Timidthy. Sodoman with the
help of Timidthy wrote three books of our Bible. They are
Job, Psalms and Song of Sodoman. Some say he wrote
Proverbs but most of us know Paul wrote that. Sodoman had
been doomed to die in the dungeon but happened to interpo-
late a dream correctly. So the philipines chained him to the
pillow of the temple he had built. The subordinate people
came by and said prodigious words to him. They were so
atrociously devastated that they spitted on him. Sodoman
could stand no more. He wanted to sit down but he couldn't
for he was chained upright. So he pulled downward with all
his verbosity, validity, and vitality, and then like a miracu-
lous miracle, the pillow fell and with it the whole temple.
This set off a change reaction all over Jericho. The buildings, the walls, the fortiments, the people - everything fell -
even Sodoman with all his elasticity. Yes, the great
Sodoman had deviously succumbered at the age of 962, a
truly stupendous man to study about.

Soloman Sleeps

I dreamed that I was on a throne
Of jewels rare, and gold,
And that the world was all my own
And I had wealth untold.

A lowly commoner did bow
And say, "My lord and king,
I would that you would tell me how
The little birds do sing."

I said, "My sir, don't question me
On myst'ries of the wood,
For I can't hear a word you say"
(Nor would I if I could.)

A peasant entered in my court
And said, "My lord and king,
I would that you would tell me how
The little birds do wing."

I said, "My sir give ear to me.
I know not how they fly
For I am blind and cannot see
The birds up in the sky.

Soloman Sleeps *(cont.)*

Just then a serf was ushered in.
Who said, "My lord, have grace
and tell me, when the pheasant's cooked,
How it does smell and taste.

I said, "My subject, I know not
The answer to your words
For I can neither smell nor taste
The sav'ry-looking birds."

And then some nobles graced my court
And said, "Our lord and king,
You are the wisest man on earth
To know not simple things.

"For every person has his view
On common things of life,
And if you set a kingly rule
This land would writhe with strife."

They tried to gain my favor long
In many wordy ways.
At last I handed them a note:
"I cannot hear a word you say."

Some believe life is a complete sentence,
Death the period.
Others think it a phrase
(dots before, no caps, dots after).

Someone Has Said

Someone has said You love me
I wonder how they heard
Perhaps, a fortune teller
Or, yet, a little bird.

It matters not who told it
I wonder if it's true.
If they would only prove it
I'd say I love you too.

But yet no proof do give me
And I will say it still.
"I love you how I love you
And yes I always will"

And answer not in whispers
Your eyes and lips can tell
For words have proven mighty
But actions mighty well.

Somewhere the Sun is Shining

Somewhere the sun is shining,
Somewhere the skies are blue.
Somewhere the Gypsy's calling,
The Gypsy's calling you.

O ramble I must ramble
Far from the haunts of man.
O wander I must wander
Into a distant land.

I see the rolling Danube,
The water's blue and clear.
The river takes my worries;
The breezes dry my tears.

From graceful old Vienna,
To mystic Budapest,
My life is but a journey:
A traveler without rest.

Budapest, Hungary

Song for the Lord's Day

Mrs. McGinley sits on the front row of church each Sunday
Singing the words that she thinks she is living
While a sign in her downtown restaurant is loudly proclaiming
"We Reserve the Right to Refuse Service to Anyone."

You know John Hayley the Sunday School superintendent.
He wears the squeaky black wingtips and red striped tie
And he's long been known for the truth that he's always been
    telling.
Such a shame that his day-to-day living must be a lie.

You know Mrs. Hartmann she teaches the girl intermediates
To be like Mrs. Hartmann the girls wish could be their fate.
But her daughter had a child illegitimately.
Could it be that she started her teaching a little too late?

Of course you remember the lad we called
    Milton Scarborough,
The tall handsome lad who always sang in the choir.
He said that Christians ought not to be in war killing
And he took his own life when the church members
    called him a liar.

Take up your cup and drink with me, to all of our hypocrisy,
To all the Mrs. Hartmanns, McGinleys, and Hayleys we know–
But if you cannot bring yourself to drink a drop of it,
Remember to pick up your mask when you start to go.

Suicide

As I stand in the place,
I can almost see your face
as I recount the final scene
I now understand what it means —
Beyond a tragedy – disgrace.

My body seems so very old.
My hands are unusually cold
Realization?
Imagination?
The house has finally sold.

Can you imagine my horror?
I aged immensely.

I could not decide if you had been
as pale and ghostly as you were then.
Had you been ill? (I did not know.
I had not looked that closely, though.)
The guilt of some impardonable sin?

The kids could not decide if you
had been this way or if it were new,
acute. They were so kind to me
They didn't indict me openly
or tell me what to do.

But, ah, I think it's very clear
Without a doubt, without a tear
your hate for me has caused your death,
although you loved me more than yourself.

Sunset

I saw one day a golden sunset
Ling'ring in the ev'ning sky.
I wanted long to hold and keep it
But the eve of night was nigh.

Sadly all the rays of sunlight
Crept away to other realms,
And the ship of Night was anchored
With Darkness resting at the helm.

Susan, 26 Years Later

At this point, it seems irretrievable.
The circles of our Venn diagram
only intersect at our children---
and that skirtingly.
I know I am defying odds and reality;
but a long look fails to see
all the chugholes and divots.
Today is like the tall grass
bent by a heavy rain:
immersion is so close to drowning.

You're in some implacable stronghold
of your will, and I am an intrusive
glint of light, an echo of
obsession, a subterranean
tunnel of forbidden notions.
Every time I approach you the
grating of vertical bars descends
with a reverberating clang that says:
"Keep out!" "Off limits!" "Do not enter!"
but what is subconscious exacts the
greatest energy: the suppressible but
uncontrollable.
You have built promising paradigms
on crystal stilts above your
reservoir of memories, dreams and passions.

Listen, a man with desire can be taught how
but a man who knows how doesn't
necessarily need the desire.

Dust accumulates in window sills
that have been closed through the seasons.
Like people they wait for a torrential
rainstorm to wash them clean.

Then follows the velvet breeze
wafting a clean fragrance and
gently drying the cisternal tears.

A parallax of visions haunts our
best-engineered plans. Who is to
say which is the more inspired?
the more arbitrary? The more
precipitous?
Sometimes the specter runs beside us
as if on a parallel track but with
warp speed. He exerts a
Venturi effect, a magnetism,
like looking over the ledge while
trying to keep the car off the edge.
It's like the life we could be living
versus the one we are living; the person
we *are* versus who we could *be*.
(It's convenient parentheses at the
ends of our **emphatic** sentences.)

You're visualizing the canyon and the
sunset and their pristine goodness.
Your focus is rich, and heartier than
ever before----
and I pushed you there.
Who could wish more than me
for your success?
I don't want you to be a failure in anything.
That's why I still pursue you.

The 60's

The decade of the sixties was a chaotic time. Few
people survived it without psychic scars and indelible
memories. It was a time of altruism and paradoxical
introspection and egoism. It was a time that threatened
the very security of this nation and the world. It was a
time of individualism, of anarchy, of mob behavior. It
was a time for honesty, a time for baring of wounds and
intentions. It was a time of iconoclasm, of irreverence,
of frustration. It was a time of idealism and violence,
and renunciation of prejudice and hatred.   It was a time
when truth was espoused by many but denied by many
more who chose to perpetuate their outmoded and
inhuman defense mechanisms. It was a time when one
was astounded over and over by the genius and again
by the barbarism of humankind. Few survived that time
without lasting memories. Some did not survive.

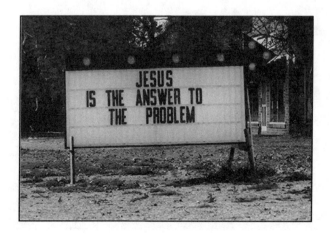

The Anti-Friend

Ask me any question and I'll tell you any answer
"I have become all things to all men..."
I'll remind you when to take your medicine
and to smile
and if I have time
I'll assist you in anything
I'm interested in.
If you need me for any reason between
8 and 5, just give me a call.

The Artist

A thought, a notion, or some sight
Fomenting in the morning light
A curse or talent from the womb
Demanding exit in the room
Before the coming of the night

So up she goes with key in hand
No recourse: yield to the demand
It has its lure like vintage wine:
The smell of oils and turpentine
in alcian sky; sienna land

Gossamers lace the varnished door
from ceiling tile to squeaking floor
And fall with whispers from their loft,
with cries as quiet as velvet's soft
to where they were before.

The rattle of the rustic key
arouses mouse community
Who scamper to their cubbyholes
and settle down as quiet as moles;
peer out uncertainly.

The opening door creates a gust
propelling clouds of gentle dust
Precipitating many a sneeze
From those assembled, if you please
No ill effect I'm told and trust.

The wash of light into the room
displays a sort of solemn tomb
But one swift pull on heavy drapes
exposes underlying capes
Erasing darkness and the gloom.

The Artist *(cont.)*

She sets the paints upon the stand
and takes the pencil in her hand.
The dormant fingers, nails are clean
No splotch of brown or wrinkled green:
She has, she will, she can.

A slash of black outlines the form:
conception, labor, soon it's born.
O bitter joy, sweet agony
to render this task accurately
and not delete, obscure, adorn.

With sweeps and scrawls
and dots and swirls
the pent-up genius now unfurls
in greys and black;
in white and brown
No smile, no voice,
no sigh or frown;
Deliberately the form goes down.

A splash of color from the brush
disturbs the momentary hush.
Forgotten feelings of the mind
Confirm uniqueness of one's kind;
explode the surface with a gush.

Deep breathing, a convicted sigh;
Beyond the point of asking why.
No longer can the fervor wait
The time has come to paint, create —
or else to die.

The Birds

I've always been enchanted
by birds who stop to sing
and tell me very shortly
that soon we will have Spring.

And though there may be snowdrifts,
and ice upon the eaves,
The birds now they have told me
and them I shall believe.

The Captain and the Cook

A funny tale was told to me
About a ship that sailed the sea,
Whose captain was a funny man
Who never could do aught but stand.

You see one day he cursed the cook
Who really b'lieved in the Good Book
And so with just a little shove
Cook pushed the captain on the stove.

The captain ran and leaped the side
In fact he really boiled the tide
In fact he lost a little hide
In fact he nearly died..

The cap came looking for the cook
Who'd jumped the side he hadn't took
Who'd laughed so hard he couldn't look.
His life he saved, his job forsook.

And now the captain steers his ship
But ne'er a curse is there to slip
The devil was burned out of him
And, praise the Lord, the cook could swim.

The Carver of a Figurine

The carver of a figurine
Sat lame beside his hut
And many charming, wistful dreams
From skillful hands were cut.

He looked upon the healthy crowd;
Compared them with his leg,
So withered, yet he still was proud
To be alive to beg.

Years came and went; he labored more
And cut and smoothed and made
The little shapes beside his door.
On mats of grass he laid.

He sold these charms and begged for alms
And time did come and go.
His hut decayed beneath the palms —
Old age and wrinkles showed.

The skillful hands of yesteryear
Were gnarled and trembling so.
His time of rest was growing near;
His form was stooping low.

His sight was bad, his health grew worse;
His work now dull and crude.
His pieces showed the old-age curse.
His stomach yearned for food.

The Carver of a Figurine *(cont.)*

He fasted long and spent his health
To live on frugal means.
He loved his charms, forgot himself,
And died amidst his dreams.

When he was buried, with his works,
In rags down in the ground,
A fortune in his humble hut
Beneath a mat was found.

The Coming of the Night

The casement's eerie glow now strode
Through tapestries of blood-red hue.
The burning embers matched the light
Of setting sun and sparkling dew.
The chimney swifts did fill the sky
And circle o'er their place of sleep.
The dreaded bats did dart and fly
On tawny air so quiet and deep.

The wind did revel in her dreams.
No rustle came from bush or tree.
The earth was mute and deaf and dark,
And only I could hear or see.
My blood did curdle in my veins;
A tingling rapture filled my spine.
I longed for wind and light and rain;
For summer days my heart did pine.

The chilly vapor of the dusk
I felt within its mystic spell.
There was no reason to distrust
The signs and scenes I knew so well.
The dying ember faded fast
And darkness covered one and all.
Into the depths of time she passed
And cast to us her old black shawl.

The Do Nothing Say Everything

Catch a stone upon your shoulders
Carry it the whole day long
Sleep with it upon your chest
Yet some say you are not strong

Stop a war that would kill many
Fathom yet the deepest lies
Find a truth where few have been
Yet some think you are not wise

Many think and yet do nothing
So they won't be criticized
And that's what they are — just
nothing
Their being – none will realize.

The Dog Run Over by the Road

There lies a dog; what dog lies there?
His master, oh, does he not care?

What laid him there, I think I know.
It was not done with malice though.

What dog lies there to ne'er reach home;
Never to bark again and roam?

Whose master knows not that he's here:
His shaggy friend, a friend so dear.

At home beside a crackling fire,
An autumn day – the heart's desire.

He thinks of hunting episodes –
And one run over by the road.

The Faded Lustre

O stand, you stalwart of the ages,
Who once did bear a lustrous sheen,
Now silent with the hope of sages,
Be never heard and yet unseen.

O stand, and murmur to the breezes
The myst'ries that your crown conceals,
And hope that when all conflict eases
Some severed band of love may heal.

O soon your status may be broken,
and all the freedom known will cease;
That cankered face would only token
A once, blue, tranquil bay of peace.

Stand tall, stand tall, we fill your hallways,
These corridors blood-stained and loved,
And we shall be there now and always —
'Til fairer worlds call from above.

The Farthest Star

Lord, I'm sitting here
and thinking about you
and how you might perceive my life
and how many things I've done wrong
When you wanted me to do them right.

O, Lord, I bless you
and Lord I thank you
for bringing me this far,
If I could stand beside you now
I could see the farthest star.

So many disappointments come
and I have been so sad,
So many worldly things I've tried
Have ended up so bad.

But, Lord, I know that you were there
All of the time you loved and cared,
You brought me right along
This way so very far.

And if I were with you now,
if I were standing there,
if I were by your side,
if I were still your child.

I could see
Oh I could see
I tell you I could see
As clear as day
I could see
Oh I could see
The twinkling of that
The glimmer of that
The shimmer of that
The beauty of that
The miracle of that
lovely, faint
but oh so bright
and purest light

Oh so very far
Oh so very far
Oh so very far

The beauty
The glory
The wonder
The splendor
of that farthest Star.

The Graveyard Caper

The six teenage boys entered the gloomy graveyard with reluctance but nevertheless with boldness and determination. They looked forward to a night of Halloween fun - although it was not Halloween.

This large graveyard might be like any other graveyard except there was an eerie, noxious vapor which pervaded every part of it - the fresh, flower-covered graves, the old ones covered with deep clover, the iron fence, - and even the crypt. The crypt was never visited, nor had it been for almost fifty years. About 1915 or 1920 the last body was placed there. Then, they started doing it a more inexpensive way; putting them in Mother earth. It was decadent, true, but that was not the only reason no-one went near it. There was a deep marsh which separated it from the rest of the graveyard and somehow, amidst moss, vines, and undergrowth, it had been, you might say, forgotten. When the Van Deflin family saw how low the ground was around the crypt, they bought a family lot on a mound in the graveyard. However, they kept paying homage to their relatives interred in the crypt - until that humid, polluted, water from the river encircled it. Even then, they went periodically, but at length the older members of the Van Deflin family died out and the younger ones moved away.

The boys stepped lightly around the tombstones for a while and then, becoming accustomed to their anachronistic playground, they frolicked demoniacally. They played Dracula for a while and even more childish games such as Hide- and-go-seek, to the fenced limit of the graveyard but never beyond the marsh.

The Graveyard Caper *(cont.)*

Then, they grew bolder. They laughed at being afraid of a harmless graveyard, sacred as it was, - and decided to frighten the living daylights out of someone. The opportunity came. It was Mrs. Jones, and she was hurriedly walking home with some items from the grocery. She really had no fear of that way to her house, though. The sidewalk was well-lighted and the graveyard - she was afraid of it. But she would walk by it real fast, as always and, of course, she would hear or see nothing.

After that, the boys split up. Three went down to the western end of the graveyard and the other three idled to the eastern end. There they planned to give any passerby the scare of his life.

When she was halfway past the foggy graveyard, there was a blood-curdling cry from deep in the opaque night. Her heart seemed to drop down into her stomach. That first terrible cry was followed by a series of painful moans and groans. Mrs. Jones fled. Terrors undreamed of entered her mind and she never stopped running until she reached home.

In this midst of their fractious fun, a car stopped in front of the graveyard. It became apparent that it was a policeman. Mrs. Jones must have called the police. The three boys on the east end hid in a tangled growth along the fence. From their hiding place, they watched the officer. Actually, it was so dark they followed his flashlight. Several times the light swept by them but they kept low. Knowing that if they ran the policeman might see them, the three boys crouched breathlessly still.

The Graveyard Caper *(cont.)*

The officer stayed in one place for a long while, surveying the damage. He took a few steps toward their car, seemed to change his mind, and then began walking toward the marsh. He traversed the length of it, inspecting the undergrowth and looking ever so often at the deteriorated old crypt. Perhaps it was a childish fancy or maybe duty but, nevertheless, he began stepping gingerly through the marsh toward the inconspicuous tomb.

The three watched all the time, breathing easier now, but saying nothing to one another. They watched and that was all. The policeman was to it now; shining his flashlight into dark, forgotten crevices. What could have been his thoughts as he paused, motionless, peering at those gored bodies and skeletons and inhaling that persistent penetrating stench of half a century? Then, to the three boys' vision another form came into view behind the officer. It pounced heavily upon him before he could turn. There were a few yells from the policeman and then he was dragged into the old crypt. Even inside his cries of torture pierced the night.

The three boys stayed in their cache for a while --- until they saw their counterparts running toward them.

"Hey, we've really had a great time haven't we?" said one of the three boys who had been hiding.
"Yea!" They all chimed in.
"Don't you think y'all went a little too far, though?"
"What d'ye mean?"
"Clubbing that officer and pulling him into the old crypt."
"Us? We thought it was you! We've been down on the other end since we split up! We thought it was y'all . . ."

The Greatest Motivator

The King of Glory became a person and experienced rejection. He was even despised. Rejection is the greatest wound, the greatest motivator for self-deprecation. It leads to low self-esteem and cynicism in the same breath. The slaughterhouse turns out edible flesh as an aftermath of the screaming bloodbath. Rejection can help us to excise undesirable elements to make us more palatable. We may not submit to the operation and continue a living death of bitterness and dejection.

The Guest

Here within a priestly palace
Aged walls are wracked with gore
And the full and silver chalice
Shall be lifted nevermore.

How outside the storm was raging
On that dark and dreary night
While inside the guest was laughing
Gloating o'er the candle light.

And its flame did flit and flicker
On that hapless trav'ler's face
Oh how dreadful to have entered
Such a hopeless, helpless place.

How the hosts tried to show interest
Fleeting smiles they often feigned,
But outside the wind did whistle
And with fear their hearts were strained.

How the wind assailed the shutters
Gaining volume all the while
And outside the bats did flutter—
Still the guest retained his smile.

Yea, in all he kept on talking,
Talking, but they did not hear
For their ears were deaf with thunder
And their hearts were torn with fear.

The Guest *(cont.)*

Oft they traded furtive glances
answered by the raging night
And the room displayed phantasms
Of the dancing candlelight.

Still he talked without an answer
And the hosts stared back at him.
Yea, the candle wax grew shorter
And the room was ghastly dim.

Yet he spoke, but grew he hoarser
And no one heard what he said,
for, inspecting very closely,
He found that they all were dead.

The Highwayman Revisited
Apologies to Alfred Noyes

The wind was a torrent of darkness
among the building roof tops,
The midnight breeze was blowing from the south.
And the gangster came speeding –
speeding – speeding –
The gangster came speeding up to the apartment house

He had a funny shaped hat on his head
A long trenchcoat around him
He walked with a stealthy tread
And hidden in his scabbard beneath his coat
was a 45 caliber colt.

Over the concrete walk to the apartment house
He walked with a stealthy tread.
He banged with his fist on the apartment door
But nothing could be heard within
He whistled a tune to the window, and
Who should be waiting there
But Jess, the landlords' daughter
Plaiting a dark red love knot into her long black hair.

And in a dark hidden alley
Behind the apartment house
There was Sam the janitor
Listening to the conversation
Crouching as quiet as a mouse
One kiss my lovely sweetheart
I'm after a bank tonight
But I shall be back with a million
before the morning light

Yet if they press me sharply and harry me through the day
Then look for me at midnight
I'll come to you at midnight
Though a hundred cops should bar the way.

He rose upright on some garbage
He could scarce reach her hand
But she lowered her hair out the window
His face burnt like a brand as the black
cascade of perfume came tumbling over his chest
And he kissed its waves in the moonlight
Then he ran to his car in the moonlight
And sped away to the west

He did not come at the dawning
He did not come at noon
And out of the tawny sunset before the rise of the moon
When the street was a speeding freeway
cutting toward the north and south
Some other gangsters came speeding
speeding, speeding up to the apartment house.

They said no word to the landlord
They drank his beer instead
But they gagged his daughter and bound her upright
to the foot of her narrow bed.
Two of them knelt at her window
With pistols getting their bead.
There was death at one dark window
For Jess could see through her window
the street on which he would speed.

They had tied her up to attention
With many a snickering jest
and had trained a pistol on her
the landlord's black-eyed daughter, Jess.
Now keep good watch and they kissed her
She heard the dead man say
"Look for me at midnight
I'll come to you at midnight
Though a hundred cops should bar the way!"

Then cold on the stroke of midnight
She strained her ears to hear
The screeching sound of tires
clearing the corners near
Screech, screech! Had they heard it?
The screeching of the tires sounding clear.
Screech, screech, were they deaf they did not hear?

Down the speeding freeway
Coming from the south
The gangster came speeding up to the apartment house
He stepped out of the car
She had to let him know what was about...
And then she let out a muffled shout
A pistol shot rang out!

He jumped in his car and sped toward the west
He did not know who stood
With her head bowed drenched in her own red blood
In the paper the next morning he read

The Highwayman Revisited *(cont.)*

How Jess the landlord's daughter had lain
dead
as he sped away.

Back he sped like a madman shrieking
A curse to the sky,
With the highway fading behind him
And waving his pistol high!
Blood-red was his hat in the golden noon
Blood soaked was his once white trenchcoat
When the cops shot him down on the highway
Down like a dog on the highway
He lay in his car on the highway
drenched in blood from his feet to his throat

And still on a summer night, they say
When the wind is a torrent of darkness
blowing from the south,
The gangster comes speeding –
Speeding – speeding –
The gangster comes speeding up to the apartment house

Over the concrete walk to the apartment house
He walks with a stealthy tread
He bangs with his fist on the apartment door
But nothing can be heard within.
He whistles a tune to the window
and who should be waiting there
but Jess, the landlord's daughter,
plaiting a dark red love knot in her long black hair.

The Killer

There are not hands to hide my face
Enough to keep me from disgrace
There are not words to change my name
and hope that things could be the same
as once.

There is not soap to wash the stains
of blood that on my hand remains.
There are not prayers to ease my mind
and help me all in all to find
my sanity.

There is no way to hide the glass
in which my grim reflections pass
There is no way to ease my health
for everyday I kill myself
as I killed someone else.

Port Angeles, Washington

317

The Legacy

He asked if my father was a doctor as he lay on the table, trusting me to remedy his coronary situation. He was looking for some confirmation that I might possess some intelligence or skills genetically or environmentally that might put him in good stead.

"No," I answer, "he was just a carpenter... and my mom is a housewife." The fact that I'm not from over-sophisticated roots might actually make him more comfortable.

The first time I was asked that question, which incidentally may be prompted solely by benign curiosity, I almost apologized for being a doctor with respect to my heritage. However, I did not realize the full legacy of my parents with respect to medicine until recently.

My two daughters are talented in visual arts. I was thinking how they came by that honestly. Their mother is quite an artist as was a paternal great aunt. My youngest daughter also writes poetry as do I and as did her great aunt.

Then I reflected on my own parents. My father was a gifted craftsman. He was thin but wiry and used all sorts of ingenious methods to give him a mechanical advantage. He primarily worked by himself, whether it was painting a steeple, roofing a house or putting in a floor. He always had a No. 2 pencil behind his ear, sawdust in his nostrils, white paint speckles on his glasses and a steady assortment of cuts and bruises on his hands and arms.

He carried extendable rulers, plumb lines with blue chalk, T-squares and the ever-present level. His precision painting was not unlike that of an artist. He lived in a world of structure, form, color, symmetry.

Of course, my girls were endowed with some of that! And so was I! Here is a man who used his hands every hour of the day to technically accomplish his mission. He was a surgeon of wood and glass. Additionally, his occupation was often dangerous: scaffolds several stories high; steeply

318

slanted roofs; remodeling virtually condemned buildings. This courage, I believe, can carry over to the offspring, perhaps, for different endeavors.

My dad used to have a quote for me when I would occasionally work with him: "This'll wear out an old man and kill a young man." His willingness to commit to hard physical and technical work is an important legacy.

My mother is also an artisan. She can make the most beautiful clothing, sew the straightest stitch, and always win blue ribbons on her pear and plum preserves. Working with her hands is a major occupation throughout the day. Her seamstress precision is no less than amazing for a lady 78 years of age.

Also, she is the most compassionate person I know. That sensitivity and empathetic capacity are also profoundly important in the healing profession and in the visual arts.

I suddenly became enlightened as to the hereditary endowment I possessed for achieving success in the technical realm. The proclivities and achievement of my children were then no less surprising.

It makes me say, "Thank you, Mother; thank you, Daddy, for working with your hands." Thank you Aunt Addie for the poems and the paintings. Thanks Mom for the compassion and the intensity.

Then when I'm asked again, "Were some of your folks doctors?", I can answer a confident "No, thankfully, for you and for me."

The Life We Live

The life we live
will someday meet
the turns we missed
upon the street.

For some we missed
we shall be sad
and yet for others
shall be glad.

The Light in the Dark

Once wand'ring lost was found by God
Within a dark'ning wood.
Once in an evil sinner man
The Lord did find some good.

Once blinded long was made to see;
Once deaf was made to hear.
One eye a lighted forest saw;
Sweet sounds fell on an ear.

And ere the sun had hid its head,
The moon did show its face.
And ere the stars could briefly shine,
Warm dawn did light the place.

A new life born; an old one dead:
New sights, new hopes, new goals —
Abandoned drink; reviving bread
And faint, but glowing, coals.

The Little Fish

There was a little fish (I'm told)
Within a silver brook,
So foolish young and bold
He bit upon a hook.

The little fish was caught
And flung onto the bank.
Oh, how he flopped and fought
With many a hearty yank.

But still the hook remained
So firm inside his mouth;
So sad was he and pained
Til it was taken out.

The fisher held him tight
Inside his calloused hand,
And with a futile fight
The fishy eyed the man.

The man began to laugh;
With hearty voice laughed he
Then opened wide his hand
And let the fish go free.

The happy little fish
Did swim away from land.
How very good it was
To be back home again!

He now afraid to roam,
Vowed not to go afar,
And safe and sound at home,
Was eaten by a gar.

The Man Who Made Al Capone Look Like
A Kid From Kindergarten

Mr. E. Deadman was executed today at the California State Prison. He snatched the Bible out of the priest's hands and spit on it as a last scene of his gruesome acts. A one-day extended sentence was denied by the California governor, James Heartless.

Among Deadman's charges were: five murders, two women strangled and three men shot; 11 grand larcenies; 32 petty larcenies; four auto thefts; drunken driving 91 times; disturbing the peace 112 times; perjury and arson; 16 armed robberies; prison escapement five times; possession of a deadly weapon 31 times; 14 assault and battery charges; intent to kill eight times; moonshining and bribery; selling narcotics and obscene literature; embezzlement, forgery, counterfeiting, trespassing, loitering, kidnapping, impersonating an officer; contempt of court; using vile language in a church; harassing people on a bus; indecent exposure; spitting in a supermarket; income tax evasion; selling alcoholic beverages without a license; breaking windows; threatening people on the telephone; being an accomplice to an interstate fugitive; and stealing candy from a child.

Thank God he's gone.

The Man Who Shot the Strausberg

Calmly he had stepped before the celebrated abstract painting "Lines" by the hermit artist Hans Strausberg. Out of his cloak he had taken a pearl-handled derringer and had put a sound hole through the centre of the painting. Then, he had placed the small pistol in an ash depository and, unhindered, had walked toward the museum exit. People were awed, offended, and surprised. For a brief second, no one moved. Then the curator and a few male art lovers restrained the suave gunman.

"What are you doing, you fool?" the curator cried.

Some of the museum visitors idled over to the penetrated painting while the others encircled the bland gentleman.

"Why did you shoot that work of art? Are you mad?" a distinctly haughty epicurean asked.

To this question the cloaked man simply replied,"Hello, gentlemen."

An obese lady cried, "A line is broken! May God forgive him."

The gentleman seemed to come back into the world around him and said, "I see you like this painting."

A few said "yes" enthusiastically.

"And you, sir, have marred the beauty of this beautiful creation," said the curator indignantly.

"It is a monster!" the indicted gentleman replied. "A mixed-up, terrible, striped monster."

"Absurd!"

"Let's take him to Commissioner LeGrande."

The stately man was taken to headquarters, and hardly a word was said on the way by his three hosts.

Arriving there, our subject was escorted straight to the commissioner's office.

"Ah ha!" said Monsieur LeGrande. "And what have we here?"

"A gunman," someone said gravely.

"And who has he shot?"

"A Strausberg."

"Uh huh, and when was the victim shot?"

"Awhile ago in the museum."

"Eh bien. Is the wound serious?"

Everyone hesitated to answer and the speedy conversation slowed down. Finally the curator answered.

"Oui. You see a line is broken."

"A line broken?" Commissioner Le Grande questioned incredulously.

"Oui, it was a painting."

"Mon Dieu!" cried the commissioner. "I thought you were talking about a person."

Unabashed, the cloaked gentleman puffed on a cigar and gazed out the window.

Legrande continued and said: "Messieurs, tell me more about this..uh.. painting."

The curator took the floor and began: "This gentleman," pointing to our anonymous personage, "although I hesitate to call him gentleman, is a murderer!"

After a while the curator spoke up:

"I guess we will just have to let M. Strausberg decide that."

All faces turned to the gentleman sitting in the corner. He seemed to come back into the world of reality for he deposited his sere cigar into an ash tray. Then, calmly, he turned his swivel chair around facing his fretful audience. The commissioner wiped the smile off his face and assumed a commanding tone of voice, directing his conversation to our character.

"And why did you shoot the painting, Monsieur?"

The Man Who Shot the Strausberg *(cont.)*

"Because it was a terrible work of art, not fit to be in an art gallery."

"I might agree with ..." Commissioner LeGrande cut himself short. "And are you in a habit of marring and defacing paintings?"

"No this was a special case."

Nervously, the commissioner lit his pipe. He sat for several minutes; eyeing first the painting piercer, and then the people waiting his decision. Finally, in an undecided stammer, he spoke to the gentleman seated by the window:

"Monsieur, I do not believe I heard your name."

And in that calm, suave voice he answered: "Hans Strausberg."

Boston Massachusetts

The Master

O some celestial artist paints
    A masterpiece divine.
His painting never dries because
    It changes all the time.
A dash of black the canvas shows
    On half its aged face;
Some streaks of yellow here and there,
    A spot of red in place.
The pastels light the veil of black
    And haze the shroud of day.
A stroke of scarlet in the west
    And in the east some gray.
Broad splashes of eternal blue
    And traces here and there.
A burnt sienna for the land;
    An ivory for the air.
A sweep of purple for the peaks
    And amber for the vales.
Off to the right the scene turns black
    And on the left turns pale.
A day of painting in our time;
    A fleeting moment but to one —
Whose dripping paint brush never dries,
    Whose head is brighter than the sun.

The Morning Waits for None

Know ye who wait for the morning
That the morning waits for none
So if you've things for doing
You'd better get them done.

I once did wait the morning
But ere the morning came
I slept in bed til half past twelve;
Alas, things were the same.

Today is the day for the journey,
The day that the prize is won;
Know ye who wait for the morning
That the morning waits for none.

Sandi Scaia

The Most Forgettable Character

I started to jump off the bridge but remembered the river had dried up. I began to jump anyway and then remembered I wasn't on a bridge. I was standing on top of a fire hydrant. I decided I would jump into the path of an oncoming car but concluded that I didn't have anything to die for except cigarettes and they were killing me anyway. I then got the idea of leaping from the highest building in town but figured that my privvy would not be lofty enough to kill me. It could hurt me but who wants to be crippled for life? It was evident that I would have to die in a big city.

I caught a train to New York and arrived in that city about 4:00 A.M. I was stopped by a big, burly, obese guy while walking down a dark, dangerous street. He said that he would have killed me if I hadn't been wearing glasses. I took them off. He said that he would have killed me if I had had any money. I pulled a twenty-dollar bill out of my pocket. He took out his knife...... just then the sun came up and my face scared him to death.

It was the early morning rush hour and cars were jamming the streets. I said "Good-bye cruel world," and stepped off the curb. Crash! Bam! Smash! Boom! Bang! It was a 213-car collision and I was on the very bottom. Unfortunately, I had stepped in a manhole and landed right on top of a man at work. The blow killed him colder than a dead frog. They closed down the street and made it an auto junkyard.

I emerged from the manhole and trekked on down the street to the Empire State Building. I got out on a

The Most Forgettable Character (cont.)

ledge and a huge crowd gathered below. Fifteen firemen and six policemen lost their lives trying to save mine. They had a net below me, but I saw a hole in it. I put my big toe on the target and leaped 51 stories ----- into an Acme Sand and Gravel truck.

I heard a horn and supposed we were at the port. I hit the water like a rock. I hit the bottom like a rock. It was a three-foot deep swimming pool for tots. Just then a man came up to me and said, "Mr. U. R. Nutty, here is a cashier's check for one million dollars." I was so happy I died laughing.

The Price of Glory

I quote to you an old old story:
Sorrow is the price of Glory.
Fame is sought and it is lovely
But what sacrifice comes with it,
But what critics do accomp'ny
And what storms assail the mind.

After fame the brow is wrinkled
And no solace can one find.
There are criticisms sprinkled;
Rude intruders all the time.
And exalted heads are hoary;
That's the price, the price of Glory.

Hearken all ye heavy laden,
Famous or forgotten still.
There is a forgotten eden
O'er a long forgotten hill.
Hearken, hearken to my story
Ere you miss your chance for Glory.

The Rain

Each leaf is alive with the rain
      which pounds my heart into submission.
I leave sleep for life
      and gaze out the window of understanding.
Nothing is so new as the rain
      fresh, cool, undulating among the sore
memories of a once weary mind,
      making all subordinate to love;
washing away all fears and jealousies,
      wetting the eyelashes when hearts
          are too hard
drenching pride in nature's balance
      of equality

The Reconstructionist Night Visitor

I went to sleep on the pit group in the late afternoon. I awakened to find someone's torso moving in concert with my own; their back against my chest. I immediately thought, "How did they get in here; and up here to the third floor without me knowing?"

I thought it was you, and putting my right hand on the right breast confirmed it.

You awakened/roused and I said, "Susan, is that you?"

You said simply "yes" and sat up and moved to a different area of the couch.

I sat up and was to your left.

You said, "I just don't know whether I can talk about it."

I noticed the windows were all open and the short window curtains were dancing in a cool spring breeze rather than the January winter chill. You must have opened the windows.

I realized I was staring at you and I quickly looked at the floor, instinctively. You had always chided me for staring at you. I thought looking away might help you say what you wanted/needed to say. We were in the semidarkness.

You started to cry and then checked it: "I'm taking a course and I'm having problems with reconstruction," you said.

An odd choice of words, I thought, but an honest admission.

Then, I guess, I woke up but the reality of your presence had been palpable and pulsatile and no less real than my solitude. I was frustrated that I had awakened but, perhaps, that's all you had to say at this time.

The Search for Someone
to Lose Myself In

Receive me as your own
for I am your own for awhile,
for a night
for a century of orgasms
which will polarize your soul
into four dimensions of
rapture.
I gape at the hole I leave behind
and wonder in my mind
if maybe here
I could be lost.

The Song Without a Name
Psalm 129

O God, how can my spirit flee
From wrinkles in Thy palm?
For everywhere I feel Thy touch –
In every storm a calm.

If I ascend beyond the clouds,
Behold, I find Thee there;
And even near the depths of hell
I can't escape Thy care.

If I should take the wings of morn
And dwell within the sea,
O even there Thou'd be my guide
And Thy hand would hold me.

O if I say I'll hide myself
Within the shades of night,
Behold, my sins are known to Thee
And darkness is but light.

O search me, God, and know my heart:
Try me, and know my thoughts.
How can I but give praise to Thee
When dearly was I bought?

Thy son so pure and righteous died
Upon the cruel tree.
A nobler gift has ne'er been giv'n
Nor shall there ever be.

He slept three days then rose again,
He who saved us from sin;
Forgiveness comes from just a pray'r
Praise be to Thee. Amen.

The Sun Will Shine Again

Weep not fair maiden for your love
Whom war has taken in,
For though the skies are dark above
The sun will shine again.

Mourn not, O holy man of God,
For worlds sunk deep in sin.
There'll come a day of firmer sod,
The sun will shine again.

Take not the pistol to your head!
Your work is not in vain.
Forget the words some fool has said;
The sun will shine again.

Physician rest your wrinkled brow
That bears all human pain.
Although it does not look it now
The sun will shine again.

O farmer stand not in the field
That's washed away with rain.
Now idle not. Go home and build;
The sun will shine again.

But oh, the sun it's always free
To any kind of man,
And only this shall I foresee:
The sun will rise again.

The Toil and the Triumph

Come over San Martin,
Come over today,
For small is our number
And raging the fray.

Come here, fellow patriots,
Come here we do pray,
For surely our lifeblood
Shall soon flow away.

The cry came from Chile,
And also Peru,
Where smoke from raised rifles
Disgraced skies of blue.

And there in those countries
The birds were on wing;
For all of the hatred,
Their throats would not sing.

And over the Andes
To Martin it went,
Who long had been waiting
And knew what it meant.

Arose, then, San Martin
With bold Bolivar,
And thousands of patriots,
To travel afar.

The Toil and the Triumph (cont.)

They marched through the lowlands
And highlands as well –
Yea, over the Andes,
A high snowy hell.

The jungles were haunted
By vampirish bats
And often their campsites
Were friended by rats.

When finally their journey
Did come to an end,
Their hurting and suff'ring
Was just to begin.

Yea, they were victorious
If Peace can outweigh
The thousands who perished
Along that hard way.

O dashing San Martin
And bold Bolivar,
May Peace be thy comfort
Wherever you are.

Yea, though the years have numbered
Thy time in the grave,
Thou shalt live forever:
The God-given brave.

The Traveler Who Packed a Cigarette Instead of a Gun

B. A. Fiend walked out of his home town, Noplace, Virginia. He took a last look at the city limits sign as he stomped out his Winston that did not taste as good as it should.

After fifty miles, he was smoking a Cavalier. Later, he was running pell-mell down mountains with a package of Pall Malls.

He came to the muddy Mississippi River at Greenville. On the bridge he emptied carbon granules out of a Lark cigarette.

In the midst of his journey, during winter, he lit up a Salem and was surprised when springtime did not appear. Disappointed, he ignited a Muriel cigar. However, Edie Adams didn't come into view.

He was getting tired after 1800 miles so he started smoking Camels. To his disgust, not a camel could be seen on the desert.

He then remembered his Bel Airs and Raleighs. He already had one between his lips when he remembered there wasn't a place to redeem the coupons.

To get in the mood of spring, he lit up a Spring.

On the Colorado River he smoked Old Golds and Lucky Strikes as he panned for gold.

He made a raft and launched into the river. He was smoking a Philip Morris when he realized there was no commander aboard.

On Route 66 he caught a ride with two guys in a Corvette. At that time, he was puffing on a Marlboro. They gave him a ride to Las Vegas. There, outside a nightclub, he watched a fountain flow as he smoked a Kool.

Later, he had a fight with a man who wanted him to switch from Tareytons.

The sun was going down over the distant horizon and darkness was covering the desert. B. A. Fiend started to light up a Fatal and then realized he had run out of matches.

The Truth of the Matter

We are but puppets you should know
cast on a stage, rocked to and fro.
Yet sadder still of worser things
we have no sword to cut the strings.

We sit and speak though naught is said
and cling to hope though it is dead.
And all our desultory dreams
portray life only as it seems.

So soon the carriage rides for all
up to the castle, to the ball.
The clock strikes twelve. It's plain to see
our image was but fantasy.

The very rudiment of all life is purpose.

Our heritage is a gift that cannot be taken away
and our future cannot be
        opened 'til that day.

To sham is to deceive oneself.

The sea of our self is usually unfathomed for fear of
a catch of reality.

All daydreams are paramount; reality is the nightmare.

Our conscience is a hammer beating incessantly
at our pride.

Bury your contentions deep and forget the place.

The Voice of Silence

The river rippled, drowsy, dreaming
The moonbeams sprinkled softly gleaming
The woodlands murmured gently swaying
And all the misty pools were saying
      Sleep, sleep, sleep.
The garden paths knew dew-dropped flowers
Dripping, dripping timeless hours
Every breast was pulsing slowly
e'en the mighty too were lowly:
      deep, deep, deep.
And all was lost to me of living;
Hating, loving, wanting, giving
I guess that's why my soul was saying,
was whispering, was quietly praying
      sleep, sleep, sleep.
And skies beheld no robin winging
nor fields had ear for sparrow singing
For all was peaceful, balmy, lovely:
Stars with droopy eyes above me
      deep, deep, deep,

And then the silence woke me.

The War is Over 1865
(a Northern contemporary visits
a burial ground for Confederate dead)

Praise be to thee, immortal men,
        Who left sweet life to die for naught.
And yet no glory-rendered shrine
        Adorns the field on which you fought.

You fell beneath a treason flag
        And God with sorrow felled the wrong.
Here in this peaceful graveyard now,
        You lie where noble dead belong.

Our silence is a token now,
        And what more can we do or say?
You died for what you thought was right;
        You proudly wore the rebel grey.

There is no country strong or great
        Except that union be the aim,
But now our brothers fill the earth;
        How much was lost? How much
was gained?

We place the laurel on your graves
        And at your peaceful chambers pause–
But what is bravery in death
        If all is for a hopeless cause?

We have a nation yet preserved
        But ugly scars across the land;
And only God can lead us now
        And soothe us with His healing hand.

If we must die then let it be
　　　As "all for one and one for all";
And with this purpose clear in mind,
　　　The Lord can bless us when we fall.

Sleep sweetly now, sleep on you, Grey,
　　　For you were wrong and yet so brave;
And even you are loss to us:
　　　The Blue who stand above your grave.

Vicksburg, Mississippi

The World Not Seen Before

One night there was a world beyond
Which lingered hardly long.
One night there was a bird on wing
Who had no time for song.
But once I saw the world of peace
In dreams of life and bliss,
And somehow did I hear the fowl
Who was so highly kissed.

One day there was a world on earth
Which had no happy name.
One day there were a thousand birds
Who played a deadly game.
But never did I see the earth
In blurry realms of light,
And never did I hear the birds
Until I lost my sight.

A pagan to a sacred shrine,
A stranger to my home,
I ground out many urgent tasks
And had no time to roam.
And now in darkness I sit here
With eyes to see no more.
Though blind I see and I construct
The world not seen before.

The World We Have Lost

The world we have lost
Has never been won
For there is no vict'ry
That comes from a gun
And after the fighting
When all's said and done
We will have but less
Then when we'd begun.

The friends of the foe
Are brothers of thine
What makes you so warring?
What makes them so kind?
But fight on keep fighting
And one day you'll find
Your sorrow's not joy
Your blood is not wine

Yes one day you'll find
With a fleeting last breath
That living was really
Much better than death
That hating the world
Won't bring you much health
And robbing men lives
Will not bring you wealth

O what is the bridge
That this world has crossed
To make such a people
Be chastened and tossed?
But too late it's stopping
To count up the cost
For so busy winning
The world we have lost.

The Years of Emptiness

I go into the kitchen
to fix the evening meal
and it comes to my surprise
that the pantry is not filled
and I lie upon the sofa
a can opener in my hand
staring at your picture
trying to understand
and it goes to show
that we just can't know
tomorrow what might be
for the years of emptiness have come
and, my friend, they've come for me.

I go into the bedroom
and a dress is hangin' there
the one I got her days ago
she never got to wear
and I stare out of the window
and whisper, "Oh God, why?"
My next door neighbor's smiling
but I'm sure my tears don't lie
and it goes to show
that we just don't know
tomorrow where we'll be
for the years of emptiness they came
and, my friend, they came for me.

The Years of Emptiness *(cont.)*

I remember all the dreams we shared
how we said our love would last
how we said that we would laugh and care
in the future like the past
and my footsteps sound so heavy
within the empty room
my mind is filled with questions
as I sit here in the gloom
and it only goes to show
That we cannot ever know
tomorrow what might be
for the years of emptiness they came
and, my friend, they came for me.
Yes, it goes to show
that we cannot know
tomorrow where we'll be
for the years of emptiness they came
and they came so suddenly
When, my friend, they came for me.

There are Times
by Susan Woodfin Rogers

There are times when enough isn't,
When the room seems too small
even for the dust.
And the glasses too large, too heavy,
too awkwardly knowing.
It's then, that the faces are smeared into one
canvas covered.
With large black spots, all
merging, all talking, all moving.
The shadows aren't shadows anymore,
but ... just ... other people, and even
the silver buttons don't see me anymore.
I followed the stitching on my cuff, and it
only met itself on the other side. Sometimes,
even your toes don't smile at you.

I was little once ... I wish I still had that
pink cat that followed me everywhere.

I'm big now ... and sometimes even my shadow
stretches so far away it becomes a part of the trees.

Sometimes ... people ask you things ... and they
don't mean it - and you just smile because you're
used to it. You, your shadow, and all those big
empty glasses.

Things I Love

Rupert Brooke was a war poet of World War I. He died in the Aegean Sea campaign of pneumonia and was buried on the island of Skyros. This handsome young poet, Brooke, termed himself the great lover and, in one of his poems, listed the things he loved. I also would like to list some of the things I love.

I love to wake up to languid days of late summer when crickets and locusts raise their monotonous drones. I love a sudden refreshing thunderstorm on a hot day. I love to walk barefoot in the rain on a warm summer night. I love the soft patter of rain because it puts me gently to sleep.

I think there is nothing more wonderful than peaceful, self-redeeming sleep. I love to wake in the morning and have nowhere to go. This allows me to go back to sleep. Yes, I love rest and there is no surer sign of mental health than the ability to rest. However, I also love hard work. There seems to be no greater reward than hard work. I might say I love hard work because it lets me rest better at the end of the day.

I love sunsets which fill the sky with shades of gold, azure, rose, and magenta. I love the nippy air which comes at the close of a warm fall day. I love to hunt when the air is cool and to lie down in the dry brittle grass on the levee. While lying there, I love to watch blackbirds and ducks migrating southward overhead. I love the smell of a freshly fired shell. I love the heavy stillness at the reddish end of a winter day.

I love clean plates and saucers which are smooth to the touch. I love a peaceful meal accompanied by music. I love to be traveling into the sunset with soft music playing. I love to sing. I love happy people. I love to laugh. I love love.

Things I Love (cont.)

I love the noble companionship of a fine friend. I love to walk beside a buddy and know that he would help me in a time of trouble. I love to walk with a girlfriend and know that God surely loved man when he made woman. I love sweet perfumes. I love sparkling blue eyes and long dark-brown hair.

I love crowds of people at the carnivals. I love popcorn and bananas. I love the quiet solitude of being myself. Then, I see all the lovely things that God has made and I also know that they are good. I then love God more and more and thank Him for giving me the ability to love. These I love and more.

Think Not That War Is Near

When churls run through the streets of ruin
And men retreat in fear,
And rays of day shine on the fray,
Think not that War is near.

When rubble fills the blood-stained streets
And hapless victims lie,
And there are groans and dying moans,
Think not that War is nigh.

When terr'ble sounds of marching men
Are heard by faces glum,
And men lie slain where Peace has lain,
Think not that War has come.

When trees are blossomed not in Spring
And planted fields are bare,
And tarnished bells yield solemn knells,
Think not that War is there.

When there's no mercy for the aged
And infants lifeless lie,
And Clamor keeps the quiet asleep,
Think not War passes by.

When trees don't blossom in the Spring
And planted fields are bare
And tarnished bells give solemn knells
Think not that War is there.

Think Not That War Is Near *(cont.)*

When trampled gardens lie in shame
And sonless mothers weep
And men near death gasp long for breath
Think not that War has reaped.

When rutted roads are filled with dead
And burning buildings fall,
And all is shrouded black with clouds,
Think not that War has called.

When yawning chasms fill the yards
And grass once green is brown
And wilted flowers sadly bow
Think not War leaves the town.

When crosses white line meadows green
Where once warm days have shone
And people talk and boldly walk
Think not that War is gone.

This I must tell you of Ann

This I must tell you of Ann
She is something dear
For she knows not how to hide
Any smile or tear.

She is honest this I love
This I love of Ann
Anything I say or do
She will understand.

And this Ann, she loves to sing;
Love to sing do I
She can sing and make me laugh
She can make me cry.

354

This Time Tomorrow

This time tomorrow —
Who knows where I may be?
What could days hold: joy or sorrow?
I only know they wait for me.

This time tomorrow —
Who knows what I may be?
A liar and very much alive
Or dead with dignity?

This time tomorrow —
Who knows who I may be?
But yet will there be tongues to tell?
Will there be eyes to see?

La Push, Washington

355

Thoughts at the Sea
Pensacola, 1968

I wrote your name in the sand;
The tide washed it away—
Away, away, away,
Forever into the sea.

———————

Night has set
But days are yet
And days shall ever be
for us.

———————

The starry silence hushed the beach
And only waves of distant laughter
touched my ears.
A raindrop found its way upon my cheek
Then lost itself—
among my tears.

———————

And people sail into the sunset
and some hide their face in the sand,
But they must all come back
answered or not.

Thoughts at the Sea
Pensacola, 1968

The sea makes you wonder —
Who you are, who you've been,
What you may be.
And then again you cease to wonder
For the day seems just enough.

———————————

The sea has a space in its heart
      for everyone
Young or old it does not matter.
People come to ask many questions
but it only answers with the surf
And for many that is enough.

———————————

and most were sad
      for the sun didn't shine
but after all
      the clouds must have their day

———————————

Don't worry my friend about the time
There will be plenty
      for all you wish to do:
If God is right
We'll live forever.

Thoughts of You
Pensacola 1968

What good am I here
with no one to see?
Or perhaps is it better?

It's easy to be virtuous
When one is alone.
So like a chorus
I continue in my nothingness:
Awaiting no buses, asking no questions,
Finding fewer answers.

Thoughts of You

I laugh
But I'm not really happy:
It's very hard to laugh alone.

————————

The wind was blowing;
I wondered if it knew you
So I ran after to ask,
"Mr. Wind, Mr. Wind . . ."
but he was gone.

Perhaps it's just as well:
He might have sadder things to tell.

————————

Sometimes I think of all the things
we could have done —
And I am sad.
But then I think of all we can do—
And I am happy.
Some things never grow old;
Each day is a new beginning.
So it is – with you and me.

Thoughts of You

We probably want too much
or not enough or nothing
We probably live too long,
too short, too fast, too little.
We probably make sure of more things
than we intend and then do less
than half we desire.
We probably are human.

Trichinosis compounded with psychosis
gave John an affable topic for rapport.
Of course they asked if he were contagious
and then let him continue.

Some make it to the underside of me
and somehow I never can be rid of them.
I doubt if I can even try.

360

Three Medals
(for Pryor Wheat)

Three medals we gave him today
But it smelled like thirty pieces of silver,
For I cheered like the rest of the amphitheater
When they mentioned his blood.

And we heard how courageous he was:
He died to save the world from its Red sins.
And they told how he went out singlehanded
    and almost won the war—
But it all seemed too far away.

Words bear lies but silence holds the truth.
Too bad we won't be able to ask him,
But could it be when he forever put down his slingshot
He saw the "giant" was too big?

Could it be that time finally tore the wool from his eyes;
That in that last salty taste of life he had a revelation?:
No one really wins the game of war
For a man's beliefs aren't lost to stones, only his life.

But for a while it was glorious:
The band played "Scars and Stripes Forever"; friends
    drank to his misfortune; there was a last unseen salute;
    and someone even wanted to name a building after him.
All of a sudden I wanted to go out and kill like a Christian
    for peace too.
But then I remembered: HE'S DEAD
    (and his wife would rather *we* keep the medals anyway).

Time, Age and Courage

Time removes the burden of power
and its opportunity.
Vicariously, we look to the young
with their radial development.

We laugh out of insecurity
at their courageous idealism
and suffer sorely
for ancient cowardice.

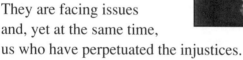

We hope they don't succeed
because we couldn't:
but more so
because we didn't let ourselves.

They are facing issues
and, yet at the same time,
us who have perpetuated the injustices.

And now, instead of fighting for justice
We are fighting because of our pride
and because, even though we are not too
old to change,
We can never be young again.

To a Fallen Leader

He lived and all lived with him.
He fell and all fell too.
He died and all mourned o'er his grave,
All lost a leader true.

From time to time we listen
As if to hear him speak.
And oft we gaze into the night
As if his hand we seek.

And in the darkened silence
Of time and tide and fate,
We light a guiding lantern
And wait . . .

San Diego Zoo, California

To Thine Ownself Be True

It will not matter: fame and fortune
    When at last your soul is due
So follow day by day your heart,
    "To thine ownself be true."

Just gold and glory will not ever
    Bring happiness my friend to you,
But yet it is a joy forever
    If one's to his ownself been true.

Some men are rich: men of sorrow:
    Followed at the chance for wealth,
While deep inside a voice was saying:
    "Thou wast not true to thine ownself."

Some have not ever heard of calling;
    Class, prestige they call success.
They count deceiving friends as more
    And truth to ones ownself as less.

I beg you friend; I pray my neighbor:
    Do not join the petty pace
Of men who light their lives with darkness
    For fear that they might see their face.

It matters not when night has ended
    Days that would not wait for you,
So long as you can say while smiling:
    "To mine ownself I have been true."

Today
words are hard to come by
so I can only smile
in the direction of
your questions.

Cummins Prison Farm, Arkansas

365

Tom Smith

The old folks said, "He's just a boy."
When Tom Smith went to war,
"Why, he don't even cuss a bit,
Or hang around the bar."
But I knew Tom Smith was a man
To leave his home and kin,
To know he might be killed in war
And not be seen again.

His father said, "I need your help.
It's time to plant, you know.
If we don't get it in the ground,
That corn'll never grow."
And Tom he said, "I know that, Pa,
But this is that way, too:
Without the help of fightin' men
America wouldn't have grew."

Tom Smith he read a lot of books
And other boys made fun.
They called him "sissy" but to Tom
It didn't matter none.
You see, Tom he was quite a lad;
A handsome fellow, too.
He seemed to know the good from bad,
The kindly things to do.

Tom Smith *(cont.)*

He donned his navy Sunday wear,
A double-breasted suit,
And neatly tucked his pants leg down
Into his leather boots.
He had to go to Coopersville,
About six miles from here.
His daddy gravely talked awhile
And tried to hold his tears.

Tom's mother said, "Oh, son my boy...
Remember to be strong."
And little Johnny said, "Hey, Bud.
Don't stay away too long."
Mrs. Smith she hugged him tight and cried;
Tom's daddy shook his hand
And said, "Be back by harvest time,
I'll need another man."

I gave Tom Smith a ride that day;
He talked and sang and grinned.
A lad so full of kindly ways,
I'd never see again.
The old folks said he was a boy
Who should be tilling land;
But when Tom Smith left home for war,
I knew he was a man.

Tommy's Song
(Dedicated to Tom South, who preached a sermon against
racial prejudice at Cross County Baptist Church 1967)

I saw you in the early morning
There were tears all over your face
You were praying for America
That God would grant her grace
The problems were so immense
and we were so intent
on their solutions:
The Vietnam war, racial strife, pollution.

And when I think back through the years
and all our fears
that we wouldn't live to see this day
Well, it makes me kind of sad
but awfully glad
God brought us all this way.

In '68 you were down in Georgia
selling Bibles door to door
and I was down in Mississippi
not sure what I was living for
And Kennedy got shot down
and all of the Nation was cryin'
and all our dreams were dyin'.

You were starin' out the window
and the record was spinnin' round and round
Dr. King had stopped his speaking
but you could still hear the sound
and you turned and you said to me,
"Have you read 'Black Like Me'
by Howard Griffin?
If you had maybe then
                    you could listen."

368

Tommy's Song *(cont.)*

The ROTC was proudly marching,
marching to and fro
and we played the "Great Mandela"
right out our third floor window
and I think about a town of 40,000
and now how not one of them is left
and the mayor of the town is Death.

Chorus: And when I think back through the years
and all our fears
that we wouldn't live to see this day
Well it makes me kind of sad
but awfully glad
God brought us all this way.

And I see you hold your children
holding them
tight within your arms
you're remembering that decade
protecting them from harm.

And Frank Reynolds is a friend
and he will be with us
til the end
When Jesus comes for us
He'll get on the bus.

Chorus: And when I think back through the years
and all our fears
that we wouldn't live to see this day
Well it makes me kind of sad
but awfully glad
God brought us all this way.

Too Much, Too Late

Don't ask me what I think of you these days.
I *don't* think of you these days
and it is contrary to my nature to lie.
I remembered for a long time
hoping the dream would come to life;
and now that *you* wish it
I'm long since exhausted with
the possibilities.
      Life to me is full of episodes
of which you can only perform in one.
That scene is long since over
and if you still remember the lines
you are a greater fool than I
for having played the part.

Toward Emotional Intimacy

This being the midterm of youth,
I desire more than fancies, frivolity, favors;
being on time; choosing the appropriate
flowers; speaking correct words; asking
pertinent questions; smiling with tenderness;
seeing the other side; dreaming together;
singing meaningful lyrics; laughing at
outworn gestures.

I long for the genuine nature of your
feelings, for what is on your mind and can
be understood, for whatever you are and will
be.

Tallulah, Louisiana

371

Trip to the
World Famous Mayo Clinic
2-22-92

Snow everywhere.
Cold like the people who are neither interested or
       friendly or who are at least guarded.
Good food, though.
And you can always learn something even if you have to
       extract it rather than absorb it.
A subway maze which quickly becomes simple and
       straightforward and is not a 'subway'.
Compulsive, tedious activities producing admirable detail
       of questionable proportions. Technically expert,
       however. The correct polished phrases
       and assurances. No banter or jest!
Suits and ties befitting a formal occasion rather than a
       roll-up-your-sleeves intervention into Mrs. Jones'
       crisis.
An expensive memory, quickly forgotten.

Turn Out the Light

Turn out the light
and let us lose our fears.
Now since it's night
our mind forgets the years.

Turn out the light;
our eyes won't look to see.
We just then might
forget that we must be.

Under the Influence of Surfak

It's the nefarious *Nebulous mysterious!*
exclaimed Dr. Procter. "Gram-variable, cocco-
bacillus, cherry slant and chocolate butt...
Discovered by a JMS (dropout) doing a tropical
medicine externship in Lee County during the
Golden Age of Parashitology ('48-'50)."

"How do you treat it?"

"The DOC is serotonin. However, there
are two unavoidable side effects: First, one
forgets everything that one has learned for the
past seven months; and, second, it prevents
erection but allows ejaculation (heretofore
thought impossible)."

"What if I refuse treatment?"

"You will invariably die and be reincar-
nated as a gnotobiotic guinea pig.(hic) You will
also possess a loreal pit. (tic)"

The choice was an easy one.

Untimely Advice

A man got murdered yesterday
In front of my house
Sat on the porch
And watched him slowly die away.

I seen the man come slipping up
With the long knife
And as I watched
I seen the poor guy's throat get cut.

The vigilantes asked around
About the kill.
They ate with us
And then proceeded over town.

They finally got their man, they did,
Oh, help him, Lord!
Inside the church.
They killed him where he had been hid.

Go kill a judge, some of the law,
A woman or
A poker player
But moonshiners, I tell you, "Naw!"

Urgent Needs

The demoniacal possessed convict
boldly bounced into the woman's bedroom
and cried "Tell me where your bathroom is quick!"
"In the house next door," she replied calmly.
"Thank you just the same." he responded,
while he stood in his mishap.

PLEASE DO NOT
ANNOY, TORMENT,
PESTER, PLAGUE,
MOLEST, WORRY,
BADGER, HARRY,
HARASS, HECKLE,
PERSECUTE, IRK,
BULLYRAG, VEX,
DISQUIET, GRATE,
BESET, BOTHER,
TEASE, NETTLE,
TANTALIZE, OR
RUFFLE THE ANIMALS

San Diego Zoo, California

VI

by Ken Helton

While trippin through a bed of squills,
A little man I chanced to meet.
A cap of blue sat on his head
And velvet slippers on his feet

He looked at me with puzzled air
As if to say I'd done him wrong;
And in a funny little voice,
He asked the reason for my song.

I laughed at him with hearty voice
And said, "Be on your way.
I'm going down to meet my love,
No time for you today."

He fixed me with that gimlet eye
Which made me feel so bare,
And said, "Because your heart is false,
Your love will not be there."

Again I laughed amusedly
And hurried on my way,
Down to the brook where lilies grow,
Where deer and fishes play.

VI *(cont.)*

I waited through the morning tide,
I waited through the noon;
And all the while I told myself,
"My love is coming soon."

When shadows from the evening sun
Caressed the ground so bare,
I thought of words heard earlier,
"Your love will not be there."

378

Watch Friend
by Ken Helton

A friend once stole my watch
Which grandma gave me for no reason
Except that is was cute
(Or maybe it was my 7th birthday, I forget)
It had Roy Rogers riding Trigger
And 'round and 'round his gunhands went
To change the minutes into hours
And hours into years

I showed it to my friend who lived
A half a block or so away
In a house beneath a hill
Of red and crumbling clay
The house itself was good for nothing
When the winter winds blew cold;
It had no screens upon the windows
The roof had patches more than shingles
And doors hung loose at funny angles
Leading onto bare, cracked floors

I was forbidden to go in there –
My keepers never told me what was wrong
With visiting my friend;
And when I told him he was welcome
To come and play inside my yard
He seemed surprised and oddly taken
That he could enter my world
While I in turn had no such chance
To share what he could offer

One day he saw Roy Rogers
Riding 'round upon my arm

Watch Friend *(cont.)*

And when I showed him the present
Transfixed he stood and watched the moments
Slipping by in precious steps
He asked if he could hold it closer
To wear it on his arm a bit;
But then he heard his mother call him
Or so he told me at the time
And off they rode into the mist

In a day or two I slipped off
To travel half a block away
To visit the forbidden kingdom
Underneath the hill of clay
And found the castle standing empty
Nothing left but mice and memories
Not good enough for me

In time my mother found it missing
And asked me where the watch had gone
I told her I had let him use it
That he would bring it back someday;
She looked at me without expression
Searching for the right words to say,
Then with delicate inquisition
Questioned why I let him hold
My most cherished of possessions

To this day I cannot tell her
The only reason I could give her
The truest thing I still can say,
I knew he was my friend

380

We Are

you are smooth

but we are smoother together

you are warm

but beds are warmer with two

you are pretty

but more so when you're sleeping

you need me

and just as lovely, i need you

We Shall Know

Take my hand
if you can
and we'll live beyond our
years
growing old
in our love
We will outlive all our fears
and when time
takes our voice
and our ears can't hear the
words
We shall know.
When there are tears
in your eyes
I will wipe them from your
cheeks
I will sing
I will cheer
I'll be strong when you are
weak
and though our eyes
may grow dim
We shall see our love so clear
We shall know, we shall
know,
We shall know.

Last night I had a dream
That we were young again
We laughed
We kissed
We cried and then we ran
and now though we touch
Well I really can't feel
but we know
yes we know
we know

What did I do to deserve myself

I was standing at the commode when a small black spider
came down in front of my right shoulder and slowly de-
scended to the yellow abyss awaiting him (her?)

I could not stop to help him or hasten him. Was it his choice
to ride some antediluvian torrent to the bowels of the earth
where big daddy or progender spiders espouse conservationist philosophy, providing sanctuaries from Chlorpyrifos. All
well and good, but how long can he (she?) hold its breath?

Has this spider been playing tuba to build up functional
residual capacity?
Or will the water dissolve its essence like the paltry plot of a
Japanese monster movie?

Why should I be concerned when I can think about crab
meat in open faced avocados and blackberries immersed in
fruit liquor and whipped cream.

(It's hard to understand sometimes how the girls I've roman-
tically kissed have become friends and some that I am barely
friends with are romantic. Does that indict my kiss?)

Maybe the spider was just space-sick. I finally concluded
that giddy weightlessness was less desirable than a gravita-
tional pull toward truth.

What is a Clear Day?

What is a clear day
that meets a reluctant world,
That's deep within its covers curled
from wakening sun?

What is a clear day
when all eyes are indifferently closed
Because yesterday's night was longer
than the dawn's dark rest could amend?

I wonder, what is a clear day
when men can't see to lift their eyes
above a stoplight into the endless skies?

Is it because we are afraid
to know how small be are?

What is a day?

What is a day after it's gone:
nothing but wisdom we should have known
nothing but deeds we should have done
nothing but victories we should have won
nothing but friends we should have made
nothing but truths we should have weighed
nothing but everything too late to know
A day is a deed that was too long ago

La Push, Washington

What is Time?
by Mark Bowles and Ken Helton

What is Time; is Love immortal?
These of truth I cannot say.
Should I taste of Death tomorrow
Of what use are these today?

Life today or Death tomorrow —
Time forever moving on:
In his fleeting, golden chariot,
Going where he oft has gone.

Rising ever like the sunrise;
Fading ever like the day,
From a morn of golden splendor
To a dusk of friendless gray.

Coming like the Hope of sages;
Leaving through the ancient door;
Pausing briefly at the threshold;
Then returning nevermore.

What Kind of World

What kind of world have we today
when people turn but look away
for fear they'll get involved?
One time they walked on every side
of a dying man
and kept their eyes straight ahead
pretending he was already dead
(hoping, at least, for the sake of their conscience)

What kind of world have we I ask
when lessons learned through countless years
have failed to penetrate our ears
because we fear the truth.
One time they spat upon the face
of an innocent man.
He said too much so they killed him
and they pretended he would never live again
(hoping, at least, for the sake of their soul)

When Tears Turn to Smiles

When tears turn to smiles
Love fades away,
Ever grown cold
Ever turned grey.

Then someday, somewhere,
When all magic ends,
The memory is but just a thought:
Old times, old things, old friends.

When There is Only One Standing

Her face is grey like folded cloths
    which keep out winter cold.
The room is dim and she makes it darker.
She is alone; more alone than ever before.
She sits in the rocking chair,
    but she doesn't rock.
Her hands are busy with crochet,
    nervously at work
Her mind a blank.
Her stare right out the frosty window
    into the darkening day.

The rain made mud and the flowers died
    just before the first frost;
Only a faded wreath reminds others.
The lights should be turned on,
    really too dark to see.
But the lights are dim, the bulbs are old.
Everything is old
    and the whole world is cold;
No one to be pleased:
No one to laugh at anything:
No one to say "I understand"
    for whatever those words were ever worth.
No one to be inattentive.
The light should be turned on.
The nights come early in winter and stay late.
The nights are so long in winter.
Oblivion too short.

When There is Only One Standing (*cont.*)

The refrigerator feels neglected;
The walls are sad and sweaty.
The picture was taken in 1933
    at Robert and Marie's.
They had just lost their baby.
The doctor said it was ...
Robert smoked to death.

Everyone liked John...
Didn't make banana pudding often enough...
Should crochet something gold,
    not too many things are gold.
Golden Wedding Anniversary:
7 more years
7 more winters
7000 long days
     longer nights
The room is dark;
The lights should be turned on.

When yesterday comes
will we still touch tomorrow
And all our hopes with one last leaf
ask time to be our friend.

Where are the Supermen?

Where are the supermen?
They are all dead.
The myth lives on in our minds
Not in our sight.
It is only fitting they should be;
Realism demands it.
For if there were live supermen
We could not hallow the dead.
If there should be no glory in death
Then there would be no cause
worthy of death.
No war which equals peace.
Such a thing contradicts tradition
Therefore it is sin.
Live sinner, or dead superman,
which do you choose to be?
It is your life. You make the decision,
But remember this:
All the supermen are dead.

Where They Pipe In Sunshine

All of us children were real good.
We hoed that cotton and chopped that wood.
We milked the cow and fed the hogs
And walked across old bogs on logs.
We worked in fields from morn 'til night.
When we got home we were a sight.
Then we would eat grits and corn pone
And later rest our weary bones.
My Pa, he was a good ole man
He dipped and spit into a can.
He once missed, and my cat turned tan.
Pa said we did not work enough,
That we were puny and not tough.
Brother Homer did not agree
And said to Pa, "Just try and see."
Big brother Jim took o'er the show.
Pa dared and Jim gave him a blow
And Pa swallowed his tobacco.
That stomach blow made it go down
And then Pa coughed and turned around.
He said, "Jim boy, since you're so tough,
We'll see about that playing rough!"

Well Pa caught Jim right by his ears
And twisted them 'til it brought tears.
He grabbed Jim by suspenders then
And tossed him into the pig pen.
Jim got up from the mud and slop
Then slid back down and said, "Now Pop,
These 'spenders sure will need sewing."

At that time we were ho-hoing
So loud that ole man Harold
Came running with his double barrel
Out of his little shack of tin.
(That was a real deluxe thing then.)
Jim had just climbed out of the pen
When thun'dring came the billy goat
A snortin' with his head real low.
He caught the seat of poor Jim's pants
And butted him over the fence.
He landed in the water trough
Then surfaced, sputtered, and he coughed.
And dripping wet he said to Pa,
"These pants sure will make good patches."

We looked at Jim and laughed and laughed.
He pretended to take a bath.
And then Ma arrived at the show
From Aunt Eva's on the bayou.
She said, "Now Jim what did you do?
You've torn your 'spenders and your pants!"
And he just sits there in a trance.
"Well Pop he threw me in here and. . ."
Ma said "James Abernathy! Man!
You have really done it this time!"
She grabbed his ear and kicked him where
I will not mention in this rhyme.
Pa softened up and shed some tears.
He even joked about his ears.
Pa said, "Before you all get killed,

Go fetch some melons from the field."
We let out cries so loud and bold,
It would have scared Geronimo.
Ole man Harold sure was afraid
He thought it was an Indian raid
For he was wearing his long johns
When he cleared the cattle pond.
And even those were drooping down
When he set out pell-mell for town.
Oh what a sight he was that day
Half in - half out his Model A!

Why should I smile at eyes
I have not known
At faces I have not touched
If you can't smile with your heart
Why bother to wipe away the tears

Winter

Some people love winter,
The ice and the snow,
The ruddy, chapped faces
And fireplace aglow.

The cough and the sneezes,
The flu and the cold,
The dangerous steps
Too slick for the old.

The swimming holes frozen,
Trees ugly and bare,
The world hibernating
In knit underwear.

Some people like winter;
They're fools I agree.
Some people like winter —
Yes, some fools like me!

Would You Like to be Friends
3-24-90

There are many unspoken conversations between us.
Occasionally a corner of intimacy is lifted, momentarily,
and then hurriedly replaced to avoid embarrassment.
I don't know how much I can say without betraying
everything and everyone: Communications rarely end
with those involved. They have a way of proliferating and
promulgating themselves. Everyone has a confidant, who
is not always confidential, and word spreads like hot butter
or the avian knowledge of bread crumbs in a public park.
I don't want to say too much and scare you or too little and
lose you. Foremost, I want to be your friend, if that is
possible. To be honest, whatever that may be.

True friendship requires commitment for emotional
intimacy - to share the triumphs and Waterloos of life; to
nurture and exhort; share vulnerabilities and be available.

It's crying out to the other person when even God
himself seems to be deaf.

It's knowing about the dark times and being faithful as a
friend.

It's propping you up when you teeter and pulling you up
when you fall. It's carrying you when the blisters and
bunions of care have become intolerable.

It's helping you to address the past and then move on,
not to be stymied by past failures or perceived failures.

It's more than love; it's action. It's not an infatuation
with certain skills or talents. It's fidelity and fraternity. It's
an encouragement to make new memories. It's setting the
person free to be whatever they can be. It's the cue-person,
the off-stage advocate. It's not a father-figure but it is a
conscience to a degree. It doesn't seek accolade or domi-
nation, exclusivism or physical exploitation. Yet, it's not
platonic or purely philosophical. It's dynamic, heartfelt,
intense, important, even critical.

398

Would You Like to be Friends (cont.)

It has to be harnessed creatively and not destructively. Other important lives cannot be beached by the fusion.

The limits are inherent and intuitive and need not be expressed.

One must allow time for these commitments to season and solidify. The milieu of each other's lives must be explored. Much of this is mundane instead of giddy. It has to do with consistency. It must be above reproach and realistic but brave and unconditional at the same time.

It demands confidentiality, compassion, time. It can never totally understand a lot of things. It never will. It will be disappointed and discouraged at times. A lack of communication will sometimes be misinterpreted as dispassion. However, friendship is predicated on a belief that it will always survive no matter what. In the hollow nights or hurried afternoon it survives.

When you feel pushed back or put down or put off you believe it survives. It always matters; it's always important but someday it may be critical.

That's when the arbors spring to life with a thousand roses; when the fruit bears its first apricot. Friendship is not the wait for the dramatic. It's the daily journey of commitment that says "I'm here, I love you. Come what may, I believe in you."

It's finally admitting our destiny instead of running away from it. It's finally accepting our responsibility though we tried to deny it. To be a friend is to really, really care. I really care about you — friend.

399

WWI

The drooping flowers shed their tears
And all the birds had roused to fly
When came in sight so very near
A horse-drawn wagon passing by
Piled full of those who had to die

Somewhere back there now Death doth win
The soldiers by the score
Who know that life doth once begin
In crowded rooms of trials sore
And peace awaits without the door

Yesterday Paints Its Colors

yesterday paints its colors

on my face

as I try to smile

into the night

I pick up my glass of champagne with

trembling hands

and all the pretty ladies

hide their bosoms in their hair

the chandelier clinkles

and the laughter is gone

with a broken violin the dancing stops

and the harlots make up their beds

the thieves sleep at night

and I cannot escape

from tomorrow

You

As the rain drips from the trees
silence in my heart
peace in my mind
hope in my life
I have found the thing
I dreamed of so long
You.

Whidbey Island, Washington

You Can Ask

You can ask the most sincere questions
that demand the most honest and intelligent answers
You look me straight in the eye
and shoot it to me
I feel like a dunce when I don't know
how I feel
or can't express my feelings

Port Angeles, Washington

You're All Around

And with the sunrise
You come to me
To take a journey
Or sail the sea
To climb up a mountain
To echo our love down
And with the sunrise
you're all around.

And with the noon
We seek the shade
To drink our water
To eat the bread you've made
To listen to each other
Or press the "leafs" we've found
And with the noon
you're all around.

And when the sun sets
Red upon the hills
And when our laughter
Suddenly grows still
We turn with tears
To hold onto the day
But with the sunset
You've gone away
But with the sunset
you've gone away.

You're Human

When you must write and know
        Not what to write,
When you must speak and know
        Not what to say,
When it is hard to stand
        the chill of night,
When it is hard to face
        The heat of day,
You're human.

When you must fight and know
        Not why you fight,
When you must sing and yet
        Not know a song,
If something in you says,
        Yes, this is right,
And something else does say,
        No, this is wrong,
You're human.

When you do give and know
        Not why you give,
When you must do and yet
        Not ask "but why?"
When you must live and know
        Not why you live
When you must die and know
        Not why you die,
You're human.

You're Not Dealing Well with the Past
1-19-92

If this is all there is or ever will be
I can be thankful for what I've had,
for what you are to me at a critical time.
When I needed someone, I got a bonus.
I'm slow to let go and I'll be slow to let go of you,
    if I must.
But I understand: people get tired of waiting,
they get exasperated.
Life seems so clear to some - so obvious,
For others of us it's hard to know when
one part of life stops and the other begins:
    It's all meshed together.

Just remember, no one could ever care more than I.
I know sometimes that's not enough.
If it's not, I understand.
However, sometimes I'm not that good at saying
'good-bye' or even acknowledging that someone has
left by choice.
There are mountains of hurt down in me
and sometimes I just can't see beyond them.
    You've helped a lot, but I'm a slow learner.

I'm sorry you feel a wall of resistance or whatever.
It was to keep you from feeling the way you do;
    it didn't work. Did it?
Maybe you could accept me as a person who really
cared a lot; who risked a lot, who lost a lot;
and who is trying to make a comeback.
    Occasionally someone can.
When it happens, I'd like for you to be
the first to know.

You, You, You

I looked into your eyes of brown
Which sadly sparkled and I knew
My heart was charmed and filled
with love
For you, for you, for you.

I heard you speak your chosen
words
So softly like a lovely rhyme
And I longed that your ruby lips
Could touch these lips of mine.

I knew that birds and skies I loved
Could not steal all my tender heart
And that the roads and seas and
hills
Should not keep us apart.

And so I said these words so old,
It was the thing I longed to do
I looked into your eyes again
Love you, love you, love you.

Ze Bank, Ze Bank

They had walked past the old bank a million times in
boyhood. There it was: worn by time like a laundered dollar
bill. In youth the three young men had first come up with
the idea to rob the bank. I guess they were about thirteen.
All through their teenage years they kept the plan in secret.
No one suspected anything of a freckled-face lad meandering
around in the bank lobby. No one had a hint of suspicion
when a skinny, tow-headed youngster wrote a feature story
about the bank for the school paper. Nor did the science
project of a black-headed kid with locks arouse any profound
interest. They were church-going boys who came from
good families, but they still had a materializing dream:
to rob the bank.

Now at the age of twenty, they had spent some seven
years studying the old bank. They had photographed it,
analyzed it, and scrutinized it. Without their parents'
knowing, they had spent endless laborious hours at secret
meetings planning their scheme. The young men had visited
new building sites, buildings under construction and had
studied numerous blueprints in detail. At last their plan was
perfected: The perfect crime, no less than the work of a
mastermind. This was the ultimate hour. This was D. day.

After closing time, Jess Tate, the janitor, did his usual
duties, cleaning the floors, pulling the window curtains,
dusting, replacing chairs and tables..... and wistfully looking
for stray bills. He finally finished, and when he got home,
his wife asked him the reason for his being late.

"I wanted to clean her up good, Bertha", the janitor told
his spouse. "Real good."

"Why so 'specially good tonight, Jess?" she asked.
He hesitated awhile and then a smile parted his lips and
revealed his snaggled-teeth.

"I might as well tell ya. Tomorrow, I won't be workin' in that old bank."

"Jess," his wife began, "you mean after all these years you gonna quit?"

"I ain't gonna quit. I'll just be janitorin' another bank. You see it was 'spose to be kept real quiet. You know that new buildin' by Perry's Hardware?"

His wife nodded her head.

"That's the new National Bank. I turned in my old keys today."

A look of horror, quickly suppressed, and then sorrow, his wife slowly muttered. "I thought that was going to be a finance corporation."

"That's what everybody thought, but it's really the bank. A modern, slick-floor bank. They moved most of the money out last night and the rest of it after closing time today."

Then, noting the look on his wife's face, he asked "Aren't you happy?"

"Yes," she feebly replied, forcing a smile.

"I'm hungry, Bertha, what time is it?"

"Six o'clock," she answered with a trailing voice and a faraway look in her eye. "Supper's on the table."

Acknowledgements

Kennard Keith Helton is an attorney, former municipal judge, and poet in Dardanelle, Arkansas. He and his wife, Kathy, have four children. Kenny and I used to write poetry in last period study hall in high school.

Charles Wayne Winkle, EdD, is a family psychologist and novelist in Fort Smith, Arkansas. He and his wife, Vicki, have two daughters. Wayne has written a book on parenting.

Joe Nix, PhD, is Distinguished University Professor in the department of chemistry at Ouachita Baptist University, Arkadelphia, Arkansas. He is a naturalist and conservationist. He is currently with the Ross Foundation of Arkadelphia, Arkansas, doing philanthropic work; and teaching land ethics to children. He and Laura, his wife, have one daughter.

Bart Pullen is a high school social studies teacher and football coach in Earle, Arkansas.

Susan Woodfin Rogers is an artist from Wichita, Kansas. She is married and has two daughters.

Geoff Bowles, my brother, has an art education degree and is retired from the Air Force. He and his wife Doris live in Stratford, Oklahoma where he has an appliance repair business.

Thanks to Angie Tomlinson, MetroGraphics, for her help and perseverance in the assembly of this book.

Epilogue

Dear Kind Reader,

I would like to humbly apologize for any poetry that espouses notions of ageist, racist, sexist, educational or socioeconomic biases. Also, please forgive any implications of discrimination against those physically, mentally, emotionally or spiritually disadvantaged.

Certainly, I am no more than the product of God's grace and must bow in awe to His blessings on my life.

Some of the earlier pieces are unsettling to me as they seem to devalue life. I personally feel that all life is worth the struggle, worth preservation to allow restoration, reconciliation, healing, regeneration.

My prayer for you would be that you find God; learn to truly know Him and His will for your life.

Sincerely,
Mark Howard Bowles